permission to shine

PERMISSION TO SHINE

Copyright © 2005, Mark Cullen

Unless otherwise stated, Scripture quotations are taken from the NLT, NEW LIVING TRANSLATION, Wheaton, IL: Tyndale House Publishers (1996).

Scripture quotations noted The Message, or Msg, are taken from THE MESSAGE. Copyright © 1993, 1994, 1995, 1996, 2000, 2002, 2002. Used by permission of NavPress Publishing Group.

Scripture quotations noted NKJV, are taken from THE NEW KING JAMES VERSION of the Bible. Copyright © 1979, 1980, 1982, Thomas Nelson, Inc. Publishers, Nashville, TN.

Scripture quotations noted NIV, are taken from the HOLY BIBLE: NEW INTERNATIONAL VERSION©. Copyright © 1973, 1978, 1984 by International Bible Society. Used by permission of Zondervan Publishing House. All rights reserved.

Scripture quotations noted LB or Living Bible, are taken from the LIVING BIBLE. Copyright ©1979, Tyndale House Publishers: Wheaton, IL.

Scripture quotations noted TEV, are taken from TODAY'S ENGLISH VERSION of the Bible (also called GOOD NEWS TRANSLATION). Copyright © 1992, American Bible Society: New York

Scripture quotations noted NASB, are taken from the NEW AMERICAN STANDARD BIBLE. Copyright © 1973, Foundation Press: Anaheim, CA.

Artwork & Design: Belinda McCullough
BAM Graphic Design T. [618] 9343 5874   M. 0403 001 827

Photography by Amanda Spurling
T. 0402 446 689

Photographs of author by Gaylene Trethewey

Publisher: Mark Cullen
info@markcullen.com.au

Printed by Hyde Park Press . Richmond . South Australia . Australia

National Library of Australia . Canberra . Australia
ISBN: 0646402048

My son, Daniel

This book is dedicated to you.

May you discover what you were
made for, live your dreams
and shine.

contents

acknowledgements

This book has taken a long time to write - about five years since I first knew it had to be written! It's been a long road, sometimes frustrating, sometimes exhilarating, but all necessary I think, to arrive at this finished product.

There's a bunch of people who've been on the journey with me, whose encouragement, friendship and advice, I could not have done without.

My beautiful wife, Ali - my greatest fan and the person who puts more courage in me than anyone. I can only write about this stuff because you have allowed me to be myself and to pursue my dreams. I love you always.

My incredible son, Daniel - who along with his mum, allowed me the extra time to write, knowing that what I was doing was worthwhile. Thanks Zoomy - I love your bones!

My Senior Pastor, Philip Baker - thanks for helping me understand why writing my book is important.

Penny Webb - my earliest "believer". Thanks so much for your encouragement and belief in me.

Kelley Chisholm - thanks for taking this project under your wing. Your insight has been invaluable. Thanks for helping me shape this book into what it is today - I would have been totally floundering without you.

Peter Elliot - thanks for the editing advice and helpful suggestions.

Paul Morrison - the man who "holds up my hands". Thanks for all you are and all you do. You make me look good! Thanks for your faithful friendship and support.

The Riverview Worship Team - thanks for your faithfulness and hard work. Thanks for supporting my leadership and continually fulfilling the vision of providing a brilliant environment for people to connect with God.

Darlene Zschech - thanks for believing in me. Thanks for being such an incredible example of a life that shines. You are one of my greatest heroes.

Andrew Naylor - my friend, thanks for always being there for me. I've learned a lot alongside you, and thank God for our journey together. You are a true "shiner".

Shayle and Joy Cullen, my Dad and Mum. Thank you for the life you gave me and the Godly teaching and love that have set me up for life.

foreword

by darlene zschech

What is the desire within you? Have you allowed the desire to breathe ... to find the life that it needs to be realised? Many people struggle with knowing what it is they were born to do, and sometimes we can make it all too complicated ... God doesn't make it hard, we do! Ask yourself these things ... What am I gifted at? What do I LOVE to do? Does this desire line up with the Word of God? Can I see it for my life? Will the purpose of my desire build the Kingdom of God?

Psalm 37:4 tells us that God clearly longs to give us the desires of our heart. He longs for it. Desire is such a powerful force in our lives, planted there by God to cause us to follow our dreams. To direct our lives and propel us toward our God-given destiny (Eph 1:11).

The Bible says that God has placed eternity in the hearts of men (Eccl 3:11). We all know there is more to life than we are now experiencing. Our hearts yearn for it. Part of this "more" is the longing to fulfil the desires of our heart, to achieve our dreams, to fully become the person we know we were made to be.

God wants us to see our dreams fulfilled yet He knows that we need to become the person who can live out those dreams. A six-year-old-boy may want to be the President of his country when he grows up. But for that dream to be realised he'll have to become the man who can handle the responsibilities and pressures of such a position. He'll have to develop in character, confidence and skill, and he'll have to prove himself many times over before his dream is achieved. And the good news is - all this can be done!

That's what this book is about: giving yourself permission to pursue the dream that is in your heart, taking the raw materials of desire, obedience and having faith in a God who is totally and utterly besotted with you. It's about becoming a big person, a whole person, the person God made you to be.

You were made to shine!

With all my love,

Darlene.

Darlene Zschech

preface

I would love to be more creative and more productive. I'm also passionate about helping others realise and express their own particular creativity and see it flourishing. I want to see a world abundant with God-glorifying artists, writers, movie makers, actors, dancers, musicians, singers, comedians, sports people, speakers and ministers.

My desire as I write this book is that it will touch thousands of "blocked" creative people - those who have suppressed their desires and repressed their creativity. I hope you find it easy to read, fun to read, and full of helpful thoughts and ideas for overcoming circumstances, habits and thinking that stop us from being who we are meant to be - who God created us to be - the person we will be most fulfilled being!

I want to inspire you - stir your desire, give some compelling reasons to pursue and perfect your God-given giftings and talents. Perhaps more importantly, to help you remove some of the fears and excuses for not chasing down the calling on your life.

The desire of my heart is that this book will help you to realise the incredible potential God has planted within you, or at least to find the confidence to take your first steps towards it.

My prayer is that you will find it inspiring, releasing, permission-giving, enlightening and full of the touch of God. My hope is that you will discover, and be bold enough to live out who you are and what you were born for.

Please don't just read this book. Interact with it. Make it your own. Write in it, underline, and highlight your favourite parts. Let it inspire and motivate you.

Do the exercises. Take the time to think and dream. Allow yourself to be pushed past your fears into the adventure of your life. Let this book be a companion on your journey.

Light up the world!

Mark

Mark Cullen

introduction

we're born to shimmer; we're born to shine.
SHAWN MULLINS

Everyone loves a person who "shines"! Someone who truly excels in a particular area, and in doing so, touches our lives with something positive and inspiring.

We were all designed to shine, and if only we would take up the challenge, overcome our fears, and believe we were born for something special, the word "average" would be of use only to mathematicians and statisticians and could never be applied to people!

For someone to shine in life presupposes that they are living successfully. But what is true success? I believe the recipe is different for each person. God has an individual plan for every life - a unique "destiny" for each of us. Success, then, involves finding and living out that unique plan, discovering that, as we do, we are deeply fulfilled, richly satisfied, and that others are touched through us by the finger of God.

For most of us, the greatest obstacle we will have to overcome before we can shine is our own thinking. What we believe determines how we behave. So our attitudes and beliefs, our angles on life, are very important indeed. Throughout this book we'll explore what I believe to be effective approaches to thinking that will lead to effective actions, and eventually a shining life!

Shining

If we are to truly shine in life, we must understand - and believe - that God has good plans for us and for what we do. We need to be comfortable with our calling - not just knowing what it is, but fully embracing it and living it. To shine we have to realise our potential through passion, hard work, perseverance, discipline and right thinking.

A glowing life requires more than great technique or highly developed skills. Many can "do the stuff" and do it with dizzying proficiency, but fail to "move" people. What we do must be infused with love.

People who shine have a "live to give" attitude. They use their gifts to touch, enhance and enrich the lives of others. They are not self-focussed or self-absorbed, but live generously, always prepared to add value to someone else's life.

Permission

Everybody wants to succeed. The truth is, most people want you to succeed too. They're not out there hoping you'll trip up or run into disaster. They'll be happy to see you do well. The best news is: God wants you to have success. He's given you permission and all that you need to achieve it.

What I have observed in many people and have experienced myself, is that we often find it hard to give ourselves the permission to succeed. We can't believe that we should achieve or experience success or outstanding achievement. That's OK for others, we think, but not us. Who are we to think that we could be incredible and enjoy the prosperous outcomes? We don't really deserve it.

There are two kinds of obstacles that can block our ability to succeed and shine: external and internal. The external obstacles are to do with the circumstances and environment we find ourselves in, and the people with whom we associate. These kinds of obstacles are quite easily recognised and so can be dealt with as necessary. We are all "victims of circumstance" to some degree, but why not design our own circumstances?

The internal obstacles are woven into our thought patterns and attitudes and are disguised by time and habit. These obstacles are much harder to recognise in ourselves. They are also generally deeply ingrained and hence harder to remove.

Throughout this book we will confront some of these internal obstacles, and at least gain some awareness of the type of obstacles that are holding us back. If we can identify and acknowledge that we have a problem, we are half-way to solving it.

I know you want to be a person who shines. That's why you picked up this book. God has given you permission and I'm cheering you on, so read on and discover for yourself the Permission To Shine.

calling
a purpose to shine

PART ONE

the journey commences

PURPOSE

A Purposeful Life

Most of us at some time in our life ask the questions: What am I here for? What am I supposed to be doing with my life? We all have an inkling deep inside that our life is supposed to be unique and deeply imbued with purpose. Some people seem to find that purpose and fulfil it while others do not.

Perhaps Jesus himself asked these same questions. We couldn't be sure. We do know, however, that somewhere along His life's journey He did find the answers to them. He was about 30 years old when He made this statement: *"The Spirit of the Lord is upon me, for he has appointed me to preach Good News to the poor. He has sent me to proclaim that captives will be released, that the blind will see, that the downtrodden will be freed from their oppressors."*[1]

Jesus knew exactly what he was supposed to do with his life. He knew that he was anointed, and why.

To be anointed means metaphorically that you have been specifically appointed and given authority to carry out a particular task. It also means that you have been given what you need to accomplish it.

The Apostle John tells us that we each have an anointing - our own unique anointing from God.[2] We have our own calling to follow and fulfil. To be able to shine truly in life we must find that calling, embrace it, and live it out passionately.

MY CREATIVE JOURNEY
A Personal Story

Some of the clearest signposts we'll ever find pointing towards the calling on our lives, are the desires of our hearts. Yet many of us are afraid to fully explore the roads they direct us down.

For example, in my life, music was deeply rooted in my heart from the age of ten. I loved (and still love) playing the guitar, coaxing a sound from wood and steel that can touch your soul, filling the air with a feeling, creating an atmosphere. I guess I was enamoured with the mystery and power of music, its ability to bypass the mind and go straight for the heart. Some have called it the language of the spirit. Being able to play put a little of that power in my hands in some way, but never the keys to the mystery.

When I had completed high school and it was time to decide what to do next, I had no idea of what I wanted to do. (Well, actually, I did. But for a number of reasons, my deepest dream didn't register as one of my options for the future.)

I began looking for opportunities that would give me the training for a "good" job or career. Something safe. Something that would pay well and be secure in the future. Something that would allow me to get married, have a family, buy a nice house, two cars, have a cat and a dog, and two kids I could afford to send to great schools. Like many people, I was looking for what would give me a comfortable and respectable life.

I had done well in Physics, Chemistry and Maths at school and thought I had an interest in electrical things (because I liked guitar amps!). Well, I must have convinced the interviewers because I landed a Cadetship (like an apprenticeship, only with more prestige!) with the New Zealand Electricity Division as an Electrical Engineering Officer. Wonderful!

Or so it should have been. My heart was restless throughout the three and a half years I spent gaining "experience" and a New Zealand Certificate of Electrical Engineering. I did exceptionally well in my studies but my heart wasn't in it. In fact, I am sure to this day that after I walked out of my final exam, I forgot virtually all I had studied!

The stirrings in my heart to find something to do in life that really connected with who I was, were getting louder and louder. I knew I wanted to do something connected with music. I began trying to find ways into the world of commercial radio - without much luck. About this time I came across an advertisement in a music magazine for a course in Audio

Engineering - recording and mixing music live or in a studio. I thought I'd found what I was looking for.

I had to leave my secure career prospects, my home country of New Zealand and all my family and friends, to cross the Tasman Sea and "pursue my musical interests" in Australia. What was I doing? I had walked out on so much and had stepped into the total unknown. This was a great adventure for me at the age of 20. It was exciting and engaging to my soul - because at last I was following my heart.

The excitement didn't stay, and my soul began to look sideways for a drink that would quench its desires, or rather, fulfil them. Only a few months later I had moved on, leaving the course unfinished.

In hindsight I realised that I really wanted to be on the other side of the mixing desk. I wanted to be making the music, not just facilitating it. The technical side is wonderful, but I'm more enthralled with the mystical side - actually bringing something into being, creating it out of nothing.

So once again I'd missed the true longings of my heart. I spent years wondering what my life was all about and where it was going. I was still developing my talents but was afraid to follow fully after the desires of my heart thinking that perhaps they weren't legitimate; maybe they would lead to nowhere.

I'd grown up in a Christian family, but it was about this time when I really made a firm personal commitment to follow Jesus. However, it wasn't until ten years later, towards the end of a two-year stint at Tabor Bible College in Melbourne, that I found the courage to follow whole-heartedly those twin signposts, gifting and desire.

I sensed God telling me He had made me like this on purpose. The personality traits, preferences, likes and dislikes and characteristics that made me uniquely me, were there for a reason. The desires in my heart were in some way connected to the desires of His.

I began to realise that I was a musician and God had made me that way, not to be frustrated by it, but to give expression to it and to give Him glory through it. So I enrolled in a two-year course to study music, primarily guitar. I took my first lessons and ventured down a path I'd been too afraid to walk fully before. Many times I found myself wishing that I'd had the courage to follow my heart ten years earlier.

Once I began to follow this path, things began to happen. Now I had put myself in a position where things could happen and opportunities could begin to come my way. People knew I was dedicated to my gift and my craft. They knew I wanted to work in music and so they thought of me when opportunities arose. Now I was mixing with people who could help advance my musical career. My time was also structured to be more open to opportunities. I was learning new things and practising, and so I improved as an artist. This brought with it confidence and a sense of fulfilment.

Over the next couple of years my musical gifts found more and more opportunity for expression and my expertise grew as a result. It wasn't all music and performance though, as I spent a lot of time and energy organising conferences. I remember wrestling with the innumerable details of two worship conferences and a leadership conference that would be staged in three states. I learned so much working on those projects, not only about organisation and process, but especially about working with people.

While the financial pressures of life were not yet subsiding, I knew I was on the right track and doing what I should be doing at this time. All the struggles of life were only making me a bigger and stronger person.

Interestingly, during this period I didn't know what kind of job I wanted. While I knew God had called me and that He had a good plan for me, I couldn't yet see how my musical gifts would fit into that plan. Sometimes this frustrated me immensely, but I knew I had to be patient and grow through the everyday challenges of life; God's plan was good and it would come to pass if I was faithful to Him.

I think it's important to realise that a calling is far bigger than any job, or even career, you could have. It's more about your life direction and purpose, and God may manoeuvre us through a number of jobs and situations to achieve things we would never even conceive.

About a year after I had finished my music studies, God set part of His plan in motion. My Pastor at the time, Peter McHugh, had recently spent some time with his friend, Philip Baker, the Pastor of Riverview Church, a large and thriving church in Perth, Western Australia. They were talking about their churches, when Phil mentioned that Riverview was in need of a "music person" in a part-time staff position.

Peter mentioned this to me, which seemed right out of left field at the time. I was not actively looking for work and certainly not that type of work! However, over the next couple of days this grew in my heart like a seed. I spoke about the idea with Ali, my wife, and as we discussed it and prayed about it, we felt it was a "God thing", so I asked Peter to find out some more details.

A couple of days later Peter told me he had talked to Phil and that Riverview were no longer looking for someone. I was then totally confused. I was so sure I had heard from God on this one. If I hadn't heard from God, then maybe I never had - maybe I didn't know what His voice sounded like at all. However, before the day was out, I decided to believe that God had spoken to me, and that maybe it was just a matter of timing. I asked Peter to check how things were going at Riverview whenever he spoke to Phil.

It must have been only six weeks later that Peter told me Riverview's plan had not worked out and they were again looking for a Music Director. The short story is that I pursued the position with confidence, believing that it was mine, and within a few months we left for our new home in Perth.

I began my job as the Worship Pastor for Riverview Church in May 1999, finding myself thrown completely in the deep end. I had come from a church of about half the size of Riverview, where I had been unofficially second in charge to the Music Director, to being the leader in a large church. I really had no idea of what to expect.

I quickly became aware that over the last ten years of my life God had been preparing me and training me for this particular challenge. I knew that I was now doing exactly what I was made for; I was in the right place at the right time. When you are being stretched to your limits, to know this is a very comforting and confidence-building awareness.

Of course, that was not the end of my journey, and my calling continues to unfold. Sometimes it is very clear and sometimes it is not. Part of my calling, I believe, is to help others to fully live out theirs. Throughout my journey I've learned some lessons that I hope will be helpful to you as you pursue the fulfilment that comes from being who you were made to be. So let's look more closely at how we can each discover our calling in life.

THE POWER OF UNIQUENESS

Let's look for a moment at the miracle of our uniqueness. The dictionary defines unique as being the only one of its kind; without an equal or equivalent; unparalleled. Cool! That's you. That's me.

As for me, I get by with my lightning flashes, grateful to have vast swathes illuminated however briefly. After that, it's a long walk in believing darkness.

JULIA CAMERON

This is the true joy of life: the being used up for a purpose recognised by yourself as a mighty one; being a force of nature instead of a feverish, selfish little clot of ailments and grievances, complaining that the world will not devote itself to making you happy.

GEORGE BERNARD SHAW

Why is my Uniqueness Critical?

God could have made all humans alike. Aren't you glad He didn't? Without individual design there would be no variety. No such thing as liquorice all-sorts! There wouldn't even be such a thing as intimacy. If everyone was the same and you knew one person, you'd know them all. Uniformity would bring absolute monotony. It would spell the death of creativity and any sort of vibrancy that springs from it. I'm so thankful God is into rich diversity and variation.

God has given different gifts to each of us. Each has a place and a purpose. A body needs all its parts to function properly because each part serves a unique purpose. A church or a team also needs all its parts to function properly.

> *The human body has many parts, but the many parts make up only one body. So it is with the body of Christ... But God made our bodies with many parts, and he has put each part just where he wants it... Now all of you together are Christ's body, and each one of you is a separate and necessary part of it. (1 Cor 12:12, 18, 27)*

FIRE-LIGHTERS
what lights your fire?

I feel closest to God when I am;

1. *(where?)* _____

2. *(doing what?)* _____

3. *(feeling what?)* _____

I feel good about myself when I am;

1. *(where?)* _____

2. *(doing what?)* _____

3. *(feeling what?)* _____

I feel invigorated when I am;

1. *(where?)* _____

2. *(doing what?)*

3. *(feeling what?)*

I feel inspired when I am;

1. *(where?)*

2. *(doing what?)*

3. *(feeling what?)*

I feel excited when I am;

1. *(where?)*

2. *(doing what?)*

3. *(feeling what?)*

I feel creative when I am;

1. *(where?)*

2. *(doing what?)*

3. *(feeling what?)*

I feel powerful when I am;

1. *(where?)*

2. *(doing what?)*

3. *(feeling what?)*

In answering these questions what have I learned about myself?

God moves differently through each of us. We hear from Him differently and express ourselves differently. People have different tastes, preferences and styles of relating, and therefore need to be communicated to differently.

Uniqueness brings versatility to a team. Each person has different areas of strength that give the team a broader base of expertise. Your particular gift mix makes the team stronger. Your unique experiences and insights will bring a fresh angle to a project or a problem.

Your unique style can put you in a position where you are able to make an impact and influence more people. Jimi Hendrix, for example, brought a unique blend of mastery, passion and carefree, kiss-the-sky attitude to his guitar playing. He influenced the direction of rock guitar forever.

Mother Theresa's unique approach to life had an incredible impact, not just on the poor and sick of Calcutta, but on the rest of the watching world. She had the courage to follow her calling into the most unfortunate of circumstances, to help some of the most needy people in the world. Her unique gifting and determination continue to inspire, long after her death.

There are things God wants to achieve that can only be done by you or through you. We need to be confident in our partnership with God. He believes in us. God made one of you because He wanted one! Understanding the power and the purpose of uniqueness should give us confidence to be ourselves.

Don't be afraid of your uniqueness; harness it, flow with it and use it. This honours God because you're being who He made you to be, and it will also inspire others.

Find what is unique about you. Don't be ashamed of it or embarrassed by it. Develop it and use it every day. Successful people know the power of uniqueness and make the most of it.

Insist on being yourself. Never imitate.

RALPH WALDO EMERSON

The person born with a talent they are meant to use will find their greatest happiness in using it.

JOHANN WOLFGANG VON GOETHE

ONE OF A KIND - the "u" in unique

Os Guiness, in The Call, writes;

> *But who are we? And what is our destiny? Calling insists that the answer lies in God's knowledge of what he has created us to be and where he is calling us to go. Our gifts and destiny do not lie expressly in our parents' wishes, our boss's plans, our peer group's pressures, our generation's prospects, or our society's demands. Rather, we each need to know our own unique design, which is God's design for us.*[3]

WHAT IS UNIQUE ABOUT YOU?

> YOUR PHYSIOLOGY

From the moment of conception you are one of a kind. Everyone gets 23 pairs of chromosomes and ends up with two arms, two legs and one mouth. However, the number of physiological features that distinguish us from one another is astounding. Just for a start, no two persons' DNA, fingerprints, voice pattern or eyes are exactly alike.

> YOUR BACKGROUND

No one else in the world was born to your parents at the place and time you were, with the siblings you did or didn't have. Your family and your place in it, your ancestors and the relationships you formed are yours and yours alone.

> YOUR EXPERIENCES

No one else slept in your bed and had the dreams you did. Even though thousands may have visited the places you have, none have experienced them the way you have. No one else has ever occupied precisely the same space as you at the same time. No one has seen through your eyes or felt through your skin your every interaction with the world. No one saw September 11 from the same vantage point as you. Who else felt what you did when you found your precious pet cat motionless on the side of the road?

> YOUR WORLDVIEW

Every relationship, every experience you have tints your window on the world. Parents, teachers, friends, television, mentors, advertisements - each influences how we view the world and no one else can lay claim to the same complex combination of these elements as you.

> YOUR GIFTING AND GIFT MIX

What you are good at is shaped by your God-given talents, your environment, relationships and experiences. This means that the finely woven tapestry of your abilities and aptitudes is peculiar to you. What you have to offer the world is absolutely unique!

> YOUR CALLING

As I have said earlier, we each have a unique calling. God cares enough about each individual to make them unique. But He doesn't leave it there with just a general plan for our good. He's got a specific path for us to tread and a particular potential for each one.

You will always bring a unique presence and personality to a team, to a meeting, to a party or to any room. That's the way it's supposed to be! Remember - make the most of your uniqueness. Use it to make a positive difference wherever you are and whatever you do!

You can do what I cannot do. I can do what you cannot do. Together we can do great things.

MOTHER THERESA

Since you are like no other being ever created since the beginning of time, you are incomparable.

BRENDA UELAND

GOD'S DREAM

Most of us know that God has a plan and purpose for our lives. He has one for my life, and a different one for your life. If you've been a Christian for any length of time you would have heard this repeatedly. But how often do we truly stop to ask God about His dream for us?

These are some of the things I know about His dream that apply to us all:

> Personally fulfilling

I know it includes a future and a hope. Jeremiah 29:11 says so. . . *"For I know the plans I have for you," says the LORD. "They are plans for good and not for disaster, to give you a future and a hope."* God does have a positive and fulfilling dream for me.

> God-centred

God's desire is for me to pursue Him! To search for Him, earnestly seek Him out, and find relationship with Him. He says, *"In those days when you pray, I will listen. If you look for me in earnest, you will find me when you seek me. I will be found by you."* (Jeremiah 29:12-14)

> Outward focussed

Another part of it is that I will be a blessing to the rest of humanity - to my family, my neighbours, my church, my city and even other nations. That's huge! God intends that *"through your descendants, all the nations of the earth will be blessed - all because you have obeyed me."* (Genesis 24:18) It's God's dream that I'll be a blessing to others.

> Part of a generous plan

He wants His generosity to be able to flow through me as I use the gifts and abilities He has given me. *God has given gifts to each of you from his great variety of spiritual gifts. Manage them well so that God's generosity can flow through you.* (1 Peter 4:10)

> Bigger and better than mine

Jesus said, *"My purpose is to give life in all its fullness."* (John 10:10) God's dream is that I would have abundant life - a full, rich and satisfying life now, and an eternity beyond imagination! *No eye has seen, no ear has heard, and no mind has imagined what God has prepared for those who love him.* (1 Corinthians 2:9)

36

Before we go on; don't worry if in terms of your calling you 'still haven't found what you're looking for'. If you start with this general plan you can't go wrong: Pursue God, believe He has the best plans for your life, and live to be a blessing! I believe that as you continue doing this, you will discover what you were born for and find that you have already begun to live an amazing, fulfilling life.

This is God's plan for everyone. It's good, but it's general. So what about the specific plans God has for me? What am I supposed to achieve with my life? How do I discover my unique calling?

OUR DREAMS

Most of us have dreams for our own life. There are things we want to do, experience and achieve in our lifetime. Your dream may be to keep climbing the ladder at work, to make a certain amount of money, to find fulfilling relationships, or to enjoy the life-enriching experiences of travel. We don't question the fact that we have these dreams and desires - they're just there. That's because God planted them in us.

I believe that the seeds of desire and the dreams God plants in us are exactly that - seeds of the specific dream He has for us. It's like a caterpillar and a butterfly, a tadpole and a frog, or a seed and a flower. There is a definite and powerful link between the two, although at first it may not seem likely. A seed's appearance is hardly impressive, but the potential contained within its casing is astounding! It's a mystery and a miracle. Fruit doesn't begin to appear until a plant has been set in good soil, nurtured, and passed through several different seasons. Even then, the fruit goes through a period of development before it takes on its final appearance.

And so it is with dreams. Dreams unfold.

When I was 18 one of my dreams was to play guitar on a record (this was before CD's were invented!) I thought that was the dream. I thought once I had done that I could die a happy man. Now I've seen that dream fulfilled and well and truly surpassed. More than 30 albums later, I can see that playing on a record was just the beginning. God's dream for me is unfolding and I can see further now. My dreams are now bigger and bolder. Somehow, I suspect His are bigger and bolder still.

Fully discovering God's dream for us is a lifetime occupation. As I mentioned earlier, there are certain aspects of it that we can know now, but the specifics of our calling unfold as we continue to pursue it.

All men dream: but not equally. Those who dream by night in the dusty recesses of their minds wake in the day to find that it was vanity: but the dreamers of the day are dangerous men, for they may act out their dream with open eyes, to make it possible.

T. E. LAWRENCE

We grow great by dreams… Some of us let these great dreams die, but others nourish and protect them; nurse them through bad days till they bring them to the sunshine and light which comes always to those who sincerely hope that their dreams come true.

WOODROW WILSON

Dreams versus Fantasies

We may be hesitant to seek God's plan because it might not be the same as ours. If that's the case, we need to be prepared to give up "our" dream. If it's not from God, it is false and without God's backing, destined to fail. It's a dead seed.

As we have discussed, God's plans for us are only good. We should never be afraid to seek out God's dream for us because as we fulfil His, we fulfil ours. King David's advice is perfect: *Take delight in the LORD, and he will give you your heart's desires. Commit everything you do to the LORD. Trust him, and he will help you. (Psalm 37:4-5)*

You cannot dream a dream bigger than God's one for you, but you can dream outside of it. My advice to you is, "Don't go there!" That is the place of frustration, not fulfilment.

One of the saddest things I've come across is people who seem to me to be chasing the wrong dream. They're putting their heart and soul into something that, for them, could never ever materialise.

WISH LIST
an exercise in uncovering desire

Take a pen and your journal and complete the following sentence. Let your imagination flow and allow it to become a paragraph or a page if necessary.

I wish _____ …

Give yourself permission to write as many wishes as you can think of. (Remember, it doesn't have to be realistic, you're just wishing.)

Now take some thinking time to review your wishes.
1. *Which ones are possible?*
2. *Which ones are absolutely not possible? Why? Really?*
3. *Why am I not making some of these desires a reality? Discuss this with a close friend.*

A Cautionary Tale

I knew a girl who really wanted to make a career of singing. Amy, (not her real name), dreamed of making a living out of singing. The trouble was, she didn't have a great voice. She went for regular vocal lessons for a couple of years but made little progress. Amy's singing teacher wasn't honest with her and gave her the type of encouragement that kept her coming back for more, believing that one day she would make it.

Amy was naïve about the daily life and demands of a professional vocalist. She didn't have any friends who were professional singers or musicians and couldn't tell you the first thing about the business side of the music industry. She had no musical training apart from her two years of singing lessons.

Unfortunately, Amy was in love with her own fantasy of a professional singer's life. She saw herself with an artsy lifestyle, making great money for "just having fun", people admiring her skill and work, and living a fabulous non-stop social life. Amy thought that singing for a living would bring her the acceptance she was craving.

I believe it's possible to have a false dream. A dream not placed in us by God but by our own fantasies. This can happen when, rather than looking to what has been planted within us, we look outward at others and envy their gifts or the benefits of their gifts. Such dreams are born out of our own inadequacies, our need for acceptance, and our need to feel significant. They are not born of the capacities and giftedness embedded in us by God.

I believe in dreams. I believe we should take hold of our dreams and pursue them with passion and persistence. What is imperative, though, is that we are pursuing the right dream. How tragic to have spent your life going after a dream only to discover that the ladder you've been climbing is leaning against the wrong wall!

It's a rare coincidence when someone else's dream fits you, but your own will always fit like a custom-tailored suit. It's worth any effort to find your own dream.

BARBARA SHER

What lies behind us and what lies before us are tiny matters compared to what lies within us.

RALPH WALDO EMERSON

WHO AM I REALLY?
an exercise in self-discovery

Get yourself a pen and pad of paper or your journal and take some time to answer these questions. First, go through them as fast as you can and write down the first answers that come to mind. Then, go back and put a little more time into thinking about your answers.

1. What do I live for?
2. What am I passionate about?
3. What do I really believe in?
4. What do I stand up for?
5. What do I stand against?
6. What do I know to be true about me?
7. What makes me cry?
8. What makes me happy?
9. What do I struggle with?
10. What do I long for?
11. What interests me?
12. Who interests me?
13. The kind of sport I love is
14. The kind of entertainment I like is
15. The kind of rest and relaxation I like is

When you've answered these questions, answer this one: What did this questionnaire tell me about myself?

PART TWO

lessons from the journey

DESIRE

I remember when I was ten or eleven years old, our family had a cassette tape that we would listen to often. The artist was Alex Hood, an Australian entertainer who wanted to speak positively into kids' lives. One song went like this:

Anything you want to do,
You can do it if you want to,
If you really want to,
You can see it through,
If you want to.

I have thought of that little song many times through the years and gained inspiration because it contains an amazing truth. If your desire is strong enough, anything is possible. Whether you do or don't do something depends on the strength of your desire.

An objective may appear to be out of your reach but intense desire can put it into your hand. Whether it is an achievement, a position, improved quality of living, attainment of goods, or any goal - if you want it enough, it's yours. *"Desire fuels our search for the life we prize."*[4]

Turning Desire into Accomplishment

How sad it is that some people die having never even expressed their desires! Desires need expression before they'll ever find fulfilment. We need to apply our will and take action on those deep thoughts because desire is a potent force. Without it, nothing of great significance would ever be achieved.

It all starts with desire. Desire is what drives determination. Determination will produce focussed discipline. Discipline yields results.

"What do you want me to do for you?" This was the question Jesus asked Bartimaeus, a blind man who had been making a scene as Jesus and his disciples were leaving Jericho one day. "Rabbi, I want to see." "Go," said Jesus, "your faith has healed you." Immediately he received his sight and followed Jesus along the road.[5]

Bartimaeus' desire to be whole was acted upon. He went out of his way to make sure he got in the way of someone who could do something about what he wanted.

Desire made him determined. Desire opened his mind and ears to opportunity (you see what you are looking for). Desire allowed him to push past discomfort (the embarrassment of calling out and people looking at him).

Desire will determine the way you position yourself. True desire releases faith and the energy to act on it.

Don't be afraid to admit to yourself what it is you really want. Cherie Carter-Scott describes wants as *"moments of inner truth. They are the secrets of the soul."*[6] Wants are like bobbing beacons on the sea of possibility.

Desire is Legitimate and Significant

We need to accept that the deepest desires of our heart are legitimate. First, they do exist and it's okay that they do. They were actually planted there by the One who knows the beginning and the end, who knows us intimately and has the best plans for our lives. He doesn't place desires there to frustrate or demoralise us. They are put there as clues that lead us toward the *"good works which God prepared in advance for us to do".*[7]

Secondly, we must believe that these inner longings are significant. They should not be ignored or pushed to the back of our consciousness for the sake of a "safe" life with less bumps and disappointments. They're not merely a mirage that will disappear when we get up close. They are not empty fairytale wishing. They are seeds that contain at least part of the power to bring them to fruition. As author John Eldridge says in The Journey Of Desire, *"The clue to who we really are and why we are here comes to us through our heart's desire."*[8]

Success is attainable only to those who possess the courage and conviction to say "I want it".

CHERIE CARTER-SCOTT

The clue as to who we really are and why we are here comes to us through our heart's desire.

JOHN ELDREDGE

Unfortunately, in some circles, desire has been viewed as something that could only be selfish and less than holy. Perhaps this is because desire is a mysterious and powerful thing. It can lead us to the darkest of places if we allow it. This thinking, however, would lead us to disown our desire and miss the incredible fact that these "distant lights" of desire are part of the blueprint of our being. Desires are intentional, of divine origin, and integral to our design. They will help take the two-dimensional outline of our potential and add shape, structure, texture and colour. They will take a plan and produce a reality.

Following Your Heart

Life coach and New York Times No.1 bestselling author, Cherie Carter-Scott, believes that finding *"your path to fulfilment is astonishingly simple: Follow your preferences, and they will lead you to your path. Find what brings you joy and satisfaction, and trust that it will also bring you prosperity. Find what makes your blood boil, and trust that it will also fuel your existence. Discover what makes your heart sing, and trust that it will create music in your life. In other words, find what matters to you, and trust that it is the signpost you have been looking for."[9]*

Desire by its very nature will call you out of your comfort zone. It will beckon you to cross the line into the territory of change. It will tempt you to risk what you know to discover what you only dream of. It will lead you into the land of possibility and give you the fuel to begin to do something about what you see. All this for the life you dream of living and for the promise of greater fulfilment.

WHAT DO I REALLY WANT?
an exercise in uncovering desire

Take some time to answer these questions. First, go through them as fast as you can and write down the first answers that come to mind. Then, go back and put a little more time into thinking about your answers.

1. *What do I dream about?*
2. *What makes my heart sing?*
3. *What's the best thing that could happen in my life?*
4. *Am I willing to work extremely hard for it?*
5. *Is it motivated from within, or from looking at what others have or are doing?*
6. *If I were to escape from my current life to my perfect life, what would that look like?*

When you're doing work you love it's a gift to the world as well!

BARBARA SHER

Don't ask yourself what the world needs. Ask yourself what makes you come alive, and go do that, because what the world needs is people who have come alive.

HAROLD WHITMAN

7. If nothing could stop me, I'd _____.
8. I'd like to have _____.
9. Is there something I'd rather be doing?
10. If so, why am I not doing it?

The answers to these questions might surprise you. They could give clues to desires that have been safely locked away for a long time. Sometimes the deepest longings of our soul need excavation to uncover them. Often we've hidden them for reasons we may or may not be aware of, and it can be painful to dig them up.

1. Are these questions uncovering anything?
2. Have I been neglecting some of my deep desires? Have I been avoiding or suppressing them? Why?
3. Is there any legitimate reason why I shouldn't pursue this desire?
4. What small step could I take today towards what is in my heart to have or to do?

FEAR AND RISK

It is possible to cover up or bury our heart's deepest desires. Their realisation is not inevitable or unstoppable. We may choose to overlook them or ignore them, or we may suppress them for many different reasons.

Perhaps it's because of a fear that we'll never actually touch them ourselves. Others might, but it would be presumptuous to think that we could. The fear of reaching for a dream that may not materialise stops many of us from ever embarking on the journey.

Perhaps it's because we fear that when we do touch them, we won't sense the ultimate fulfilment we are thirsting for. (This is true of course, since this fulfilment will only be realised when we meet Jesus face to face in Heaven.)

It could be that we believe we would be letting down our parents or others around us who may not understand what we are pursuing and why. It may be easier for us to live out the dreams of others.

We can choose the safe life, the stable life, existing comfortably. Many, perhaps most, do. Or we can follow the deep desires and longings of our hearts, allowing them to call us toward a richer, fuller, more meaningful life. The ride is wilder, the scenery more beautiful, the adventure exhilarating - and your heart will thank you!

The key that unlocks energy is 'Desire.' It's also the key to a long and interesting life. If we expect to create any drive, any real force within ourselves, we have to get excited.

EARL NIGHTINGALE

Twenty years from now you will be more disappointed by the things you didn't do than by the ones you did. So throw off the bowlines, sail away from the safe harbour. Catch the trade winds in your sails. Explore. Dream.

MARK TWAIN

IN SYNC

The concept of "synchronicity" is fairly widely held in the arty and New Age sections of society. Synchronicity is a term coined by Carl Jung to denote meaningful coincidence or a fortuitous intermeshing of events. Perhaps another word for it is serendipity. The basic premise is that the Universe is intelligent and responsive, acting and reacting in our interests. For example, you've been thinking about making a side step in your career so have begun to look for a course that will help you transition. Within the next two weeks you meet a friend of a friend who is currently doing the course, discover an article in your favourite magazine on changing careers, and your boss approaches you about altering your hours, which, as it happens, would work in perfectly with the course you want to take.

Long before the popularity of the "New Age" movement, this concept was often spoken of as providence and usually attributed to God's goodness. Here's what William H. Murray had to say on the subject: *"The moment one definitely commits oneself, then Providence moves too. All sorts of things occur to help one that would never have otherwise occurred. A whole stream of events issues from the decision, raising in one's favour all manner of unforeseen incidents and meetings and material assistance which no man could have dreamed would come his way."*

I definitely believe synchronicity happens. However, I don't believe it is because the Universe is intelligent and responsive. It happens because there is a personality behind the universe who is intelligent and responsive and loves people! I believe in a God who loves me, has a plan of good for my life and my gifts, and wants to help me achieve the dreams He planted in my heart! Of course things are going to *"work together for good"* if I'm following His plan for my life!

When we begin to act on our dreams and desires, opportunities begin to appear. It seems our initiative begins to unlock all sorts of favourable conditions and circumstances. We shouldn't be so surprised by this. If God has planted the desires in us, surely He is more than a little interested in helping us fulfil them. Is it so strange that we would be the recipients of His favour? We need to have a little faith that things will go our way when we follow our calling. We can step out boldly knowing that the One who controls all resource, (and is not short of supply), is backing us all the way.

UNWRAPPING YOUR PRESENTS
an exercise in identifying your giftedness

God has given different gifts to each of us. Each has a place and a purpose.

> God has given each of us the ability to do certain things well. So if God has given you the ability to prophesy, speak out when you have faith that God is speaking through you. If your gift is that of serving others, serve them well. If you are a teacher, do a good job of teaching. If your gift is to encourage others, do it! If you have money, share it generously. If God has given you leadership ability, take the responsibility seriously. And if you have a gift for showing kindness to others, do it gladly. (Romans 12:6-8)

Here are some questions to help you think about your gifts and talents. This is where it is very easy to keep moving on without really thinking about the answers. Let me encourage you to take the time to think over the questions and answer carefully and honestly. Yes, it could be difficult, but I really want you to take another step towards finding your purpose.

1. What did I love doing as a child?
2. What was I passionate about?
3. What were my favourite subjects at school or university?
4. What did I want to be when I grew up? What was the attraction?
5. What am I really good at now?
6. What do others say I'm good at? What do I get complimented for?
7. Do I have gifts that I may not have fully acknowledged before?
8. Could I take my talents and strengths more seriously?
9. Should I? YES!

> A wonderful realization will be the day you realize that you are unique in all the world. There is nothing that is an accident. You are a special combination for a purpose - and don't let them tell you otherwise, even if they tell you that purpose is an illusion. (Live an illusion if you have to). You are that combination so that you can do what is essential for you to do. Don't ever believe that you have nothing to contribute. The world is an incredible unfulfilled tapestry. And only you can fulfil that tiny space that is yours.
> LEO BUSCAGLIA

We all derive from the same source. There is no mystery about the origin of things. We are all part of creation, all kings, all poets, all musicians; we have only to open up, only to discover what is already there.

HENRY MILLER

It is a mistake to look too far ahead. Only one link in the chain of destiny can be handled at a time.

WINSTON CHURCHILL

APPRECIATING THE JOURNEY

I'm sure we've all voiced the back-seat childhood cry, *Are we there yet?…
Are we there yet?…* We all want to arrive! Many of us, as adults, are still
whining, How long till we get there? We are impatient to get where we're
going and to be who we're going to be!

Life is a journey. It's a process. That's the nature of it. It unfolds as we go
along. We can't see around the next corner until we get to it - but we will
get to it. We are carried along in the flow of this process and can't get out
of it even if we want to. So it's necessary we understand the importance
of the journey. We need to work with it and make the most of it. How we
respond to the circumstances of the journey will determine the speed and
comfort of the ride!

Dreams can come true. Dreams do come true! Every day, people are
seeing their hopes and dreams realised. They're seeing things come to
pass in their lives that they've dreamed of, hoped for and worked towards
for years. They're walking into their destiny. This can happen for you too,
but you must learn to appreciate the journey.

UNDERSTANDING DESTINY

The destination is the end point of a journey, the place at which one plans
to arrive. I wonder, though, whether we should look at destiny as being like
a magnet that, if we allow it to, draws us along the path toward it. One
'pole' of the magnet is the dreams, desires and giftedness God has placed
inside us. This impels us toward the other 'pole', our 'destiny' - the good
plans and future God has in store for us. There is an irresistible attraction
between the two, and an unfinished, unfulfilled feeling until they meet.

We see destiny partly as being the point of arrival, but a complete
definition of destiny must also include the process of reaching that point.

Destiny is like a picture we have on a wall. It's a picture God has painted
that we will have a part in completing. The closer we get to the picture, the
bigger it appears. Then as we approach the picture we realise that it's
actually a window! This is the way life works: Just when we think we're
arriving, we discover there is so much more.

As Henri Nouwen wrote, *"He who thinks he is finished is finished. Those
who think they have arrived have lost their way."*[10]

NEGOTIATING THE JOURNEY WELL

1. Don't be afraid to start!
   A journey of a thousand miles begins with a single step. CONFUCIUS
   Q. How do you eat an elephant? A. One bite at a time.
2. Keep moving! Don't stop and camp!
3. Remember every hill and valley has its purpose!
4. Draw strength from others and give strength to others!
5. Remember the end purpose of the journey is to bring blessing - to you and others!
6. Learn to enjoy the ride! Enjoy where you are now! Shine where you are now!

GROWING IN CHARACTER

Calling is a word that carries similar meaning to destiny. However, *"calling is not only a matter of being and doing what we are but also of becoming what we are not yet but are called by God to be."*[11]

Skill, confidence, knowledge, wisdom, and character are all built on the journey.

We don't suddenly become a great minister, an outstanding musician, a multi-millionaire, an incredible communicator, an amazing artist, or a powerful influencer. First we build foundations. Then we build on those foundations. Then we refine and sharpen our skills, and repeatedly do what is right.

Each step builds on the last. We learn, we stretch, we grow, and we mature, as we are patient and persistent. Sometimes we need to take it slowly and steadily, confident that God is in control and is not thwarting His own plans! Going too fast can blind us to things that are important. We can miss things that are vital to our development. It's like missing a significant maths lesson early in the year: our progress is severely hampered and we struggle because we missed a basic concept that is a building block for all future work.

Peter understood the concept of process in building an effective and God-pleasing life.

> [5]*So make every effort to apply the benefits of these promises to your life. Then your faith will produce a life of moral excellence. A life of moral excellence leads to knowing God better.* [6]*Knowing God leads to self-control. Self-control leads to patient endurance, and patient*

It's like driving a car at night. You never see further than your headlights, but you can make the whole trip that way.

E. L. DOCTOROW

Character building is a slow process. Whenever we try to avoid or escape the difficulties in life, we short-circuit the process, delay our growth, and actually end up with a worse kind of pain - the worthless type that accompanies denial and avoidance.

RICK WARREN

endurance leads to godliness. [7]Godliness leads to love for other Christians, and finally you will grow to have genuine love for everyone. [8]The more you grow like this, the more you will become productive and useful in your knowledge of our Lord Jesus Christ. (2 Peter 1:5-8)

This passage outlines the process of growing in our Christian life. Each level of maturity is born out of the one before.

No great quest or journey is all smooth sailing. Storms and strong winds will come from time to time and we need to learn to face these with courage and accept them as part of the journey. If we refuse to face issues when they come we are in danger of spending our days going "round and round the mountain" - the same mountain. If we don't learn a lesson the first time, the same issues keep recurring until we do learn. Often it's a painful and frustrating process.

James teaches us, when *"trouble comes your way, let it be an opportunity for joy. For when your faith is tested, your endurance has a chance to grow. So let it grow, for when your endurance is fully developed, you will be strong in character and ready for anything." (James 1:2-4)*

When we do encounter pain on our journey, we can take some comfort in the fact that it will actually help us. It directs. It teaches. It sharpens our thinking.

We can rejoice, too, when we run into problems and trials, for we know that they are good for us - they help us learn to endure. And endurance develops strength of character in us, and character strengthens our confident expectation of salvation. (Romans 5:3)

Many times I've had to persist through tough situations. Sickness, family issues, disappointments with people, financial strain, time pressures and work stress have all taken several swings at me and my family. But every time, if I remain faithful, I come out better equipped for the next challenge.

In Genesis 12:1-2 we read about Abram's journey:

> *Then the LORD told Abram, "Leave your country, your relatives, and your father's house, and go to the land that I will show you. I will cause you to become the father of a great nation. I will bless you and make you famous, and I will make you a blessing to others."*

It was a long, tortuous journey, both physically and emotionally. And it was filled with many dangers and confrontations, family issues and abundant opportunities to doubt. However, Abram believed God. He had faith that

If you want to work on your art, work on yourself.

CHEKHOV

If you go to work on your goals, your goals will go to work on you. If you go to work on your plan, your plan will go to work on you. Whatever good things we build end up building us.

JIM ROHN

God had good planned for him. As a result he grew and God blessed him making him a man of great wealth and influence.

THE VOICE OF EXPERIENCE
a view from the future

You may need a journal or a pad of paper for this exercise.
Imagine and describe yourself at ninety.
What has life been like for you?
What have you achieved?
What have you enjoyed?
What advice would you give a nine-year-old?
What advice would you give a nineteen-year-old?

GROWING IN INFLUENCE

The purpose of the journey is to bring blessing to you as well as those around you. Our light is designed to shine. We are meant to be great examples to others, having positive influence in their lives, leading them to a life that is better.

Whatever good we have received - whether financial, emotional, circumstantial, or relational - we should put to use to enrich and help others. We are blessed to be a blessing. This concept comes from Genesis 22:19 where God tells Abraham that through his descendants, *"all the nations of the earth will be blessed - all because you have obeyed me."*

We influence people throughout our journey. There's no particular point in time where it suddenly begins to happen. If we are shining, people will look to us. There will come a day though, when we must make the decision to make our influence intentional. We must accept the responsibility of leadership - the obligation to impact the world around us. This is all part of our calling.

Finding and fulfilling our calling is the journey of a lifetime. It's never-ending, but it does have a beginning. Sometimes it's hard to see what's down that winding road, but if we keep moving we'll soon be able to see around the next bend. The important thing is that we do begin the journey and continue to take the ride.

MY JOURNEY
an exercise in looking back

We all take the journey of life. Sometimes it's an exciting adventure, sometimes it is cruel and punishing, sometimes it can be plain boring.

Joseph's journey was astounding![12] He went from a spoilt but envied son in a large family, to a hostage in a dry and dusty hole in the ground, to a slave in a foreign nation, to the most trusted aide of a high ranking official, to prisoner, to ruler of the world's most powerful nation, to patriarch of a people! That's a long and bumpy ride! But look at the lasting legacy produced because Joseph was determined to believe in his calling and stick with it through thick and thin.

Read the biography of someone you admire and write a paragraph outlining their journey. Include any major successes or failures and life incidents. Use it to encourage you on your journey.

Write a short version of your own journey so far. What are you learning from life? What has the road taught you?

We are the fruit of the past. We are the seed of the future.

JULIA CAMERON

Many believe - and I believe - that I have been designated for this work by God. In spite of my old age, I do not want to give it up; I work out of love for God and I put all my hope in Him.

MICHAELANGELO BUONARROTI

prayer

Dear God, wise and loving - I believe You made me with a purpose in mind and that You have a magnificent plan for my life. Please guide me each day as I endeavour to live out my dreams. May they be Your dreams. I want to fulfil Your call on my life and shine for You. Amen

Commitment to Calling

I, _____, promise to pursue the reason for which I was born. I will determine my areas of strength and talent and use them to fulfil God's calling on my life. I will continually recalibrate my life to ensure I am bringing the fullest possible expression of my unique contribution to the world.

Signature _____ *Date* _____

ENDNOTES

1.   Luke 4:18
2.   1 John 2:20
3.   Guiness, Os: *The Call*; WORD Publishing, Nashville; 1998, p48.
4.   Eldredge, John: *The Journey Of Desire*; Thomas Nelson Publishers, Nashville; 2000, p2.
5.   Mark 10:46-52
6.   Carter-Scott, Cherie: *If Success Is A Game, These Are The Rules*; Bantam Books, Sydney; 2000, p23.
7.   Ephesians 2:10, NIV
8.   Eldredge, John: *The Journey Of Desire*; Thomas Nelson Publishers, Nashville; 2000, p2.
9.   Carter-Scott, Cherie: ibid p52.
10.   Quoted in *The Call*, Os Guiness, WORD Publishing, Nashville; 1998, p242.
11.   ibid p30.
12.   Genesis 37-41

creativity
producing something that shines

PART ONE

understanding creativity

THE PURPOSE OF CREATIVITY

I once had a guitar teacher who would say, *"As long as you enjoy making your music - that's all that matters. You play for yourself, no one else."* At the time I knew I didn't agree with him. Something about that kind of thinking just didn't sit right with me, but I didn't challenge him on it because I couldn't quite put my finger on why. Now, I have a very clear response to such a statement: creativity is given to us by God, not primarily for self-enjoyment and self-fulfilment, but to bring glory to Him. It is also given to touch others (by bringing a glimpse of His glory to them). We are blessed to be a blessing!

As I write this, the sky is cloudless and as blue as I've ever seen it. The grass and trees seem more alive. The air is still. This is a perfect day. God's handiwork is unmatchable. This feeds, heals and refreshes me. It strikes me that this is what God's creation does for people. Since we're made in His image, our creativity should do the same for others. If we truly find what we were made for and do it with purity, people around us will be soothed, healed, refreshed, nourished, de-stressed and inspired - just by being around us.

The Bible tells us that if we manage our gifts well, God's generosity flows through us to those around us (1 Peter 4:10). I have found this an incredibly empowering thought. God touches people through us when we are simply doing what we were made for. It makes sense doesn't it?

As we use our creative gifts and talents to glorify God and touch others, we are fulfilled and able to enjoy the act of using them far more than if we were doing it purely for our own gratification. Those who create only for their own purposes and to fulfil their own desires will not truly shine.

I want my music to glorify God. It is part of my life purpose to make Him famous! I also want my music to touch people - and not just on the surface. I want them to feel inspired, strengthened and encouraged. I want the weary soul to be invigorated and the anxious mind to experience peace. I want the fearful to be comforted and the inhibited to be released. I want the weak spirit to be empowered and the timid to become bold. I want the hard heart to be softened. I want them all to know that there is purpose and meaning to life.

I don't want all I do to be for me. I want to make an impact outside my own life, to have influence - positive influence. I want to play, sing and write to move people. As a musician, I want every note to count!

WHAT IS CREATIVITY?

Trying to define creativity is a difficult proposition. Fundamentally, it is a capacity belonging to an intelligent mind. Creativity is the child of wonder. It springs from curiosity and employs as its tools the faculties of perception and imagination. It concerns itself not so much with what is, or even what is possible, but with what could be. It actively pursues the answers to the question, "What if…?"

"If you can't imagine, you can't invent. … If you can't conceive of things that don't exist, you can't create anything new."[1] Einstein believed that *"in creative work, imagination is more important than knowledge."*

Creativity has been described as perceiving or rearranging old ideas or materials in new ways, or processing common information in original ways. As Nobel Prize-winning physician, Albert Szent-Györgyi asserts, *"Discovery consists of seeing what everyone else has seen and thinking what nobody has thought."*

Creativity sees the extraordinary in the ordinary. It makes uncommon associations and observations. It also has the ability to express or present these to others in a beneficial way that instructs, inspires or entertains.

Howard G. Hendricks defines creativity as *"the generation of unique, innovative thoughts, actions, and feelings, with appropriate implementation for the benefit of others. It often means little more than the ability of perceiving in an un-habitual way. It is a function of knowledge, imagination, and evaluation."*[2]

TAKE A DIFFERENT VIEW
an exercise in changing perspective

James Mapes said, "Learn to change your perspective and creativity explodes." Go out of your way to do some things differently. This will give you a different perspective and who knows what you may discover!

1. *Go to the city and spend an hour looking in shops that normally you would never go into.*
2. *Spend a day looking at life through the eyes of another, for example;*
   > *A photographer*
   > *A poet*
   > *A jingle writer*
   > *A Mercedes car salesman*
   > *A bird*
3. *Wear something ridiculous in public on purpose.*
4. *Try a different café or restaurant from usual. Have something different for lunch. Try something unusual.*
5. *Next time you go somewhere, go the "wrong" way.*

THE SOURCE OF CREATIVITY

The Bible tells us everything that exists was created by God.[3] The account of creation as told in Genesis chapter one tells us nothing more about God's character than that He is creative and productive and that His work is good. We are then told that God made people and patterned them after himself. God created people *"in His own image"*, which means we have the ability to be very, very creative. We have imagination, intelligence and the rest of God's creation to work with.

C. S. Lewis makes an important point about the human ability to create:

"We arrange elements [God] has provided. There is not a vestige of real creativity de novo in us. Try to imagine a new primary colour, a third sex, a further dimension, or even a monster which does not consist of bits of existing animals stuck together. Nothing happens. And that surely is why our works ... never mean to others quite what we intended: because we are re-combining elements made by Him and already containing His meanings."[4]

We create because we've been made in God's image. The creative capacity is a reflection of our Maker and is God's gift to us. The ultimate glory for our creative achievements, then, belongs to God.

CREATIVITY PRINCIPLES

Here are some principles of creativity that a Christian worldview will provide.

1. *We are created "in the image" of a creative God. Our creativity is a gift from Him.*
2. *All people have a capacity for truth, goodness, beauty and creativity.*
3. *These capacities can and should be cultivated.*
4. *The proper use of our creativity glorifies God.*
5. *God-glorifying creativity reflects truth, beauty and order.*
6. *Creativity and beauty, as with all things, exist to glorify God.*
7. *Creativity is not inherently good or evil. It can be a tool for either.*
8. *Creativity, like love, requires expression. In fact, it exists only in expression.*
9. *The expression of creativity, like truth, goodness and beauty, needs no justification.*
10. *Beauty is valuable to God regardless of utility.*

CREATIVE MOODS

Many of us don't give much thought to the importance of our creativity and the fact that we can nurture it and help it to flourish.

For creativity to flourish, it must be nourished. For it to have a future, it must have nurture.

It can be useful to think of our creative side as a separate entity with its own personality. This inner creative person has moods. It would be helpful to be able to understand these moods. How do they affect our creativity, what causes them and how can we actually influence them?

I discovered the truth of this one morning after spending an extended, un-pressured time devoted to my "creative self". I was quite noticeably more easily and enjoyably creative. Things flowed a lot more smoothly and I produced both more quantity and better quality work. My "creative" had responded to attention and nurture and was in a good and productive mood.

That one session told me, loud and clear, that if I'm regular and generous with time devoted to creativity I will be rewarded with results.

If I am consistent and substantial in nurturing my "creative", it will become confident and enthusiastic (just like any person who receives similar treatment). It will then be able to produce comfortably, grow in maturity, and eventually begin to truly shine.

Just as the weather or circumstances can affect our emotional moods, there are things that can positively or adversely affect our creative moods. Our emotional moods and our creative moods are different things, but they can affect each other.

Some things that will influence our Creative mood:
> Surroundings, physical environment
> Level of stress or calm
> Tiredness
> Sensory input (books, movies, people, magazines, experiences, etc.)
> Momentum - being "on a roll"
> Emotional state (e.g. happy or crushing circumstances)
> Physical health
> Time and "space"

I used to wonder why creative people wanted to make their surroundings comfortable, enjoyable and easy on the eye. It's as if their workspace itself is a work of art! Supposedly it inspires them. Now, with a little more experience, I think they are right. The surroundings themselves don't necessarily inspire, but they put a creative person in a mood that allows him or her to be more easily inspired.

So you see, imagination needs moodling - long, inefficient, happy idling, dawdling and puttering.

BRENDA UELAND

Creativity lives in paradox: serious art is born from serious play.

JULIA CAMERON

CREATIVE CASTLE
building a safe creative place

You may have heard the saying, "A man's home is his castle." It is the place where he feels safe and in charge. As creative people we need our own castle - a place where we feel comfortable, secure and empowered. A place we can retreat to and create in peace.

Do you have a place or area devoted to your creativity?
A chair, a room, a shed, a corner?
If not, could you make one?

What would you do?

_____

_____

_____

Do something today to make your creative space more inspiring.

Good art is a form of
prayer. It's a way to say
what is not sayable.

FREDERICH BUSCH

Make visible what,
without you, might
perhaps never have
been seen.

ROBERT BRESSON

EXPRESSION

It is crucial for us as artists to learn to detect our true feelings. We can then allow those feelings to be expressed properly and not suppressed. Somehow creativity comes along with the expression. You have to have something to express - something you feel strongly about - before you express anything. And creativity is all about expression. It's about how you express, how you show your feelings. Creativity cannot exist apart from expression. That's why fear and inhibitions are so destructive - they encroach on the freedom of expression.

To really shine we need to be expressing well; efficiently, smoothly, without effort. To begin to shine we need to begin to express. Get the stuff out there. Sing, write, play, perform… whatever - begin to do it and let it speak.

There are two parts to the "performance" of an artist. One is the mechanical and the technical: the physical act of performing. The other is what is being expressed through that performance, and why. This is more of a spiritual and emotional contribution. It is the expressive and creative part. It is what carries "emotional weight" and is able to move people. Fear and inhibitions cut off the ability to let this transcendent side flow, and we can give a performance that is no more than going through the motions.

To enhance our capacity for creative expression, we must create for ourselves a safe environment and an inspirational atmosphere: one that breeds confidence and encourages productivity and self-expression.

CREATIVE AFFIRMATIONS
an exercise in truth reinforcement

As we grow up all sorts of assumptions about creativity become lodged in our thinking. Some of those assumptions may be false and unhelpful and need to be dislodged. It may be helpful to re-programme our thinking about creativity. A good place to start is to repeat some simple truth-filled phrases.

What we repeat, we remember;
What we remember, we know;
What we know, we believe.

Here are some truths that will help us approach life more freely and creatively. Say them out loud several times a day for the next week.

1. God made me because He wanted me. He loves me.
2. God has very good plans for my life. These plans encompass my talents, creativity and productivity.
3. My future is bright.
4. I was made with an awesome capacity for creativity.
5. Being creative is natural for me because I've been made in the image of an incredibly creative God.
6. I have received great gifts from God.
7. When I use my gifts God is pleased.
8. When I use my gifts others are blessed.
9. When I use my gifts I am fulfilled.
10. God's generosity flows through me when I use my gifts.
11. I am willing to allow God to work through me.
12. I am an example to others.
13. It is important that I nurture and protect my creative gifts.
14. I will develop my gifts.
15. I will use my gifts in service to God and humanity.

Write some affirmations of your own:

1. _____
2. _____
3. _____
4. _____
5. _____

Artists are people with the gift of expression. They express life with patterns of sound, with paint on a canvas, with stories and poems.

Leland Ryken

Vocabulary enables us to interpret and to express. If you have a limited vocabulary, you will also have a limited vision and a limited future.

Jim Rohn

CREATIVITY KILLERS

Fatigue

Tiredness is one of the killers of the creative mind - maybe the greatest. It's just impossible to be creative when you're worn out. You think slower. You're far less likely to think outside the box and see things from a fresh angle. Make sure your lifestyle includes good sleeping patterns and adequate rest.

Artificial Stimulants

Some people claim that drugs can help your creativity, and perhaps in very small doses they may. (How many creative people do I know that swear they can't function until after the second cup of coffee in the morning??!!) It's usually the people using drugs who believe this and think they're being creative. To everyone else, they just look like people on drugs. Some drugs may initially stimulate the mind or body, but beyond that point will usually begin to block normal functioning. When the human body and mind are not functioning fully, creativity begins to be distorted and weak, and can even become perverted. These "creative stimulants" are really the lazy way of thinking outside the box and can lead down a path that ends up destroying creativity rather than enhancing it.

Negative Criticism

Negative criticism from yourself or from others is a killer. It closes down creativity before it even begins. Be careful to whom you show your work - especially if it is unfinished. Some people are unable to see the potential in a raw form of your work, but may be quick to see the flaws. They can shut your creativity down with as little as a raised eyebrow or a quizzical look.

Try to be easy on yourself too. Creative people are notorious for erring towards perfectionism. This can be disastrous in the early stages of the creative process. We can be overly critical of ideas and edit them before they are even fully formed. If we keep rejecting acorns we will never grow an oak.

Stress

Stress is often closely related to tiredness and overwork, which can also result in a lack of time. It generally means your mind is too busy thinking about other things to concentrate on creating. Your focus will be fragmented. Obviously this is not conducive to producing great work.

In the early stages of the creative process, the issue is not, Is it right or wrong? But Where will it take you?

Howard G. Hendricks

A new idea is delicate. It can be killed by a sneer or a yawn; it can be stabbed to death by a quip and worried to death by a frown on the right man's brow.

Charlie Brower

COMING CLEAN
an exercise for improving creative health

Two practices or indulgences that I have allowed in my life, that I know are bad for me, or for my creative life, are:

1. _____

2. _____

(For example: watching too much TV, too much coffee or coke, overspending, too much socialising, staying up too late…)

I am / am not going to do something about them because;

_____
_____
_____
_____

This is what I'm going to do:

_____
_____
_____
_____

Routine is the enemy of creative thinking.

STANLEY MARCUS

Perhaps too much of everything is as bad as too little.

EDNA FERBER

PART TWO

practising creativity

FILLING THE CREATIVE WELL

It's helpful for me to think of inspiration as being drawn from a well. Whenever I need inspiration, I dip into the well and use what I need. Unfortunately, this is a source that needs careful and constant maintenance to keep from running dry. If I am serious about living a creative life, I need to be serious about maintaining and enhancing my access to inspiration.

There are as many ways of doing this as there are people but, as with anything, there are some general principles we can all apply.

Physical Factors
NUTRITION, REST AND EXERCISE
Humans are complex creatures! We have a physical body through which all our capacities must be achieved. There are myriad reasons why our body may not be able to perform optimally. Sickness can sap the strength. Tiredness or exhaustion can also leave us lacking energy and feeling unmotivated.

Good rest is essential for our bodies to operate well. Good fuel is also imperative. A balanced and sufficient diet makes a body work well. Exercise is necessary to keep it in effective working order.

Our bodies also house the non-physical elements of our being. Our soul, spirit, mind, emotions. All of these - including the physical - have an effect on each other.

Since our greatest tool for expression is our body and all it contains, we must take care of ourselves. We must do all we can to keep the container of such treasures in pristine condition.

RELAXATION

Just like a small child or a spouse, our inner creative person thrives when treated to generous amounts of time. It will enjoy sitting in the sun doing nothing; lying on the floor with headphones on listening to music; going for a walk, riding a bike or swimming.

It's important to give yourself time to unwind and let your subconscious mind do its work. Isn't it true that your best ideas have come in the shower or while you are driving, or when you're just about to slip off to sleep? Geoff Bullock's classic song, The Great Southland, was written in a very small room on a long thin strip of soft, perforated paper!

Creative Input

There must be cycles of input and output. Like a computer, if nothing goes in, nothing comes out. Simple! I need to revive, recharge. Sleep, on its own will not do that for me. I find that enjoying the creativity of others is helpful. Seeing a masterfully portrayed movie or reading an engaging and lucid novel can take you on a wonderful journey of the mind. Listening to music that has been conceived and performed with incredible skill and emotion is bound to stir my imagination. Before long ideas are flowing and can't wait to be put into concrete form.

To let my mind be fruitful, it first must have seeds planted, watered and nurtured. Some seeds will already be hidden there, lying dormant just waiting to be watered by inspiration from the well.

The mind needs constant stimulation. It needs a steady stream of fresh input, which is then stored in the memory. Fresh sensory input often triggers associated memories that then combine with the new input. This process is what will stimulate original ideas or incite new perspectives.

Brain food must be actively sought. This is where the creative root - curiosity - comes into play. Do something new each day. Do something differently each day. Listen to a different radio station, drive to work a different way, read a magazine you wouldn't normally read, wander through a park, watch people. Keep your eyes and ears open, and taste, touch and smell things. Be aware of what is passing through your sensory gates.

It's a very good idea to always carry a notebook or a voice recorder so you can capture great ideas immediately wherever you are, while they are still fresh. Many of your notes may turn out to be less brilliant than you first thought, but a handful will be absolute gems that you will be very glad to have captured.

Brain Exercise

Just like our bodies, our brain needs exercise to keep fit. If you don't exercise your brain, it will get slow and lethargic. Read as much as you can about everything possible. Books exercise your brain, provide inspiration and fill you with information that will allow you to make creative connections easily. Always be open to learning new things - always see yourself as a beginner. Hang out with creative and intelligent people and have discussions that challenge your thinking. *"As iron sharpens iron, a friend sharpens a friend."*[5]

Be Challenged

One way to keep the creative juices flowing is to stay challenged. Never be content with what you know or what you can do. Make sure you're always actively working towards something. Confront your thinking often. Don't allow yourself to get in a rut. Be curious. Always ask, "Why?"

Challenge yourself by being exposed to the creative thinking of the masters. Read their biographies. You are bound to be both challenged and inspired by some of history's creative geniuses: Leonardo da Vinci, Picasso, Einstein, C. S. Lewis, T. S. Eliot, Thomas Edison, Mozart, Beethoven... The list is long!

GET THINKING
an exercise in self-discovery

Five things I used to love doing (but don't do much anymore):

1. _____

2. _____

3. _____

How vain it is to sit down to write when you have not stood up to live.

HENRY DAVID THOREAU

If you wish to find, you must search. Rarely does a good idea interrupt you.

JIM ROHN

4. _____
5. _____

Five skills I would love to have:

1. _____
2. _____
3. _____
4. _____
5. _____

Five things I would never do, but secretly would like to try:

1. _____
2. _____
3. _____
4. _____
5. _____

Five things I'd like to study to know more about:

1. _____
2. _____
3. _____
4. _____
5. _____

Five hobbies that would interest me:

1. _____
2. _____
3. _____
4. _____
5. _____

Something I'd like to try once:

1. _____

2. _____
3. _____
4. _____
5. _____

Human beings need structure. We all need limits to things, even pleasurable things - and bottomless, creative things more than all the others!

BARBARA SHER

CREATIVITY AND LIMITATIONS

Here's a simple but little known truth: freedom inhibits creativity. It would seem like an oxymoron but it is true. If I'm asked to speak to a group of people it helps me a lot to be given a subject; the more specific the better. To be given the freedom to choose my own subject can be almost paralysing. Where do I start? What if I choose an irrelevant subject? The task can intimidate me. It just looks too big if there have been no boundaries set.

As a guitar player, one of the suggestions for getting out of the rut of playing the same old patterns, is to limit yourself to playing with 2 fingers (or even 1). This forces you to think outside the box. There's nothing like restrictions to get you thinking.

Here's a way to force creative thinking: When you need a fresh idea, open a dictionary and select a word at random. Now try to formulate ideas incorporating this word. You'd be surprised how well this works.

This can be true of time limitations too. Often the pressure of a deadline can produce great work. It forces us to actually do something!

Your art does not arrive miraculously from the darkness, but is made uneventfully in the light.

DAVID BAYLES AND TED ORLAND

BEING PRODUCTIVE

Begin to practise being productive and prolific. One of the reasons people become prolific is because they "show up" - at the page, or at their instrument, or at the place where they do their creative work. They show up without fail. They have a regular schedule. For example, Stephen King writes every single day. He sets himself a goal of 2000 words and makes sure he reaches it whether it takes him two hours or all day. Stephen King must certainly be considered prolific having produced 30 novels, as well as 19 other books, 27 movies and several television series. At least a part of the reason for this incredible volume of work is his ability to "turn up" every day.

One reason to practise being productive is that each creation contains within it the seeds of the next. If you follow the output of an artist's work over a period of time, you will almost certainly be able to discern an evolution of thoughts and ideas being expressed, as well as a progression of technical skill and experience.

It is important that we continue creating. Don't give up because your last piece wasn't a masterpiece. Even faulty creations have their purpose. They carry seeds, lessons and inspiration. Without the particular ideas that occurred to you in the process of creating your last piece, without the refinement of skills attained through working on it, what would the next piece be?

Beginning

To become productive we must get proficient at beginning. Procrastination produces nothing but frustration (and low self esteem, and … poverty). You just have to start. It doesn't have to be a perfect idea to start - you can always come back later and modify if necessary. Just get it out there and see what other ideas it stimulates.

There needs to be some movement otherwise nothing can happen. There's no direction without movement. When there are several movements in a row we get some kind of flow - and the flow can be directed. This is true for your life and it's true for your work.

JOURNAL

One thing that I believe is helpful to do, is to take time every day just to write down thoughts - any thoughts, whatever comes. About half an hour is good. Just use a journal or a school exercise book and capture some of those thoughts that float through your head onto the paper. Don't edit as you go and don't have any agenda. Just write. I don't know how this works but I believe it does from my experience. It probably has to do with the fact that it leaves "space". Life space. Space not filled with any other particular thinking. Most of the time it's just nonsense, but you'll be surprised at some of the ideas that come out. A number of the thoughts contained in this book began in this way.

Journaling is a practice that doesn't necessarily replenish the creative well, but that keeps the mouth of the well free of obstructions. It helps to keep the access to inspiration clear.

THE DISCIPLINE OF REPLENISHING

As a creative person, if I am to be all I can be, I must learn self-discipline. I can't afford not to. I can't afford not to fill my well of inspiration. I must open up the channels for creativity to flow. I can do that by devoting time to learning how and just doing it. As the great modern philosopher Nike says: Just Do It!

It comes down to priorities and the self-discipline it takes to keep them in order. I've got to be committed to becoming a more creative person. I've got to be committed to nurturing my creative self, releasing more of my creativity and creative potential. I must remember that I am a creative being, but I must order my life in such a way that I can express it to my fullest potential and allow it to flow. This glorifies God, blesses others, and brings me satisfaction.

The important thing about making room for and nurturing our creative gifts is to take lots of time. Take it from something else and give it to creativity.

I wrote this in my journal recently:

I will take time to feed my creativity by seeing movies, listening to great music, reading inspiring books and visiting museums, art galleries, libraries and other interesting places. All this I'll do leisurely. These things must soak in, seep in, infuse, so that out of my heart my mouth will speak, my pen will write, my voice will sing, my body dance. My inner creative eyes and ears will "see" and "hear" and I will then be able to bring new and significant works into existence.

We have to forge our own creative lifestyle: a way of living that includes time for creating and time for replenishing; time for input and time for output. The key to making a lifestyle is consistency. We must make creativity a part of our everyday life, not a special event.

MY OWN CREATIVE PRAYER

Take time with your pen and journal to write your own creative prayer - one you can pray regularly and from your heart. Try to keep it short and focussed. (See the prayer on the following page.)

If it takes discipline to work, it also takes discipline not to work, to allow the water level to rise until action becomes again the natural spilling forth of inner fullness.

JULIA CAMERON

Very often ideas come to me when I'm falling asleep - when the busy mind gets out of the way, and the intuitive, imaginative mind gets a shot at the steering wheel. My friend, writer William Gibson, told me, 'It's an established phenomenon. The elves take over the workshop.' That's why all writers keep a pen and paper by their beds.

DAVID CROSBY

prayer

Infinitely and magnificently creative God, thank You for choosing and trusting me with creative gifts. Help me to develop and use them in the best way possible. May they be used greatly in influencing people towards You, and in bringing honour to Your name. Amen

Commitment to Creativity

I, _____, make this commitment to value, nurture and exercise my creativity. I will take care of myself physically, emotionally and spiritually. I will stimulate inspiration by expanding my experience. I will be productive, stepping out in faith to bring into existence what does not yet exist.

Signature _____   Date _____

ENDNOTES

1. Root-Bernstein, Robert and Michèle; *Sparks Of Genius*, Mariner Books, Boston, New York, 2001, p22.
2. Hendricks, Howard G.: *Colour Outside The Lines*, 1998, W Publishing Group, www.wpublishinggroup.com, p23.
3. Jeremiah 10:16
4. *The Quotable Lewis*, ed. Wayne Martindale and Jerry Root (Wheaton, Ill.: Tyndale, 1989), p135 (italics his).
5. Proverbs 27:17

confidence

the power to shine

PART ONE

understanding confidence

Have you noticed how people who shine seem to achieve things effortlessly? They step up to the plate and perform their tasks with ease and without apology. There is no second-guessing, no question that what they are doing is not theirs to do. One of the reasons for this is their confidence.

Who doesn't dream of possessing that kind of confidence? That boldness and authority that comes from knowing what we're made for and how much God believes in us? That air of assurance that whatever happens, things will work out?

WHAT IS CONFIDENCE?

Consulting several dictionaries helps us define confidence as: *a state of mind, or a manner, marked by easy coolness and freedom from uncertainty, diffidence, or embarrassment.* Confidence speaks of people who are comfortable with themselves and their talents, as well as being comfortable with others and their talents. It involves the conviction of one's own worth or ability, an inner assurance of one's capacities and abilities. It is clear that confidence has its root in one's thinking.

WHAT IF?

Allow yourself to answer these questions:
> *What if we couldn't fail, only learn?*
> *What if there were no limits?*
> *What if the only limits that exist are ones we have made ourselves?*
> *What would you do if you knew nothing could stop you?*

The Power of Confidence

We must not underestimate the power of confidence whether it be in an individual or in a group. It is the power to achieve success. Leadership specialist, John Maxwell, calls it "the cornerstone to success". It gives energy, staying power and boldness.

Confidence is contagious. That's why it's a vital ingredient of great leadership. It carries conviction and makes others believe in you and what you're doing.

Confidence gives a "sure footedness" and conveys an aura of class. It gives you and those around you a sense of security and stability.

To express openly and with conviction requires confidence. It follows, that to create with clarity and authority requires confidence. To be able to give freely and be an inspiration and blessing to others we need to be confident.

God wants us to be confident. When He called Joshua to lead the people of Israel, He told him to be strong and courageous.[1] In other words, be confident! The command "Fear not!" is the most common in Scripture. We can be sure God wants us to live confidently! Confidence is not intimidated or easily overwhelmed. It is not apprehensive or threatened by others.

Confidence is healthy - it's not the same thing as egotism, it's not arrogance. We need it if we are to reach our potential and live out the dreams God has for us.

Confidence is a quality that can be built up or torn down. It's important to realise that once confident doesn't mean always confident. American Pro Football Hall-of-Famer, Joe Montana, said, *"Confidence is a very fragile thing"*. It's true it can be like a house of cards, especially if it is built solely on our most recent performance or achievement. However, I believe confidence that has been built on a foundation of truth and sound thinking will be unshakeable.

SHINING EXAMPLES
learning from others

Name five people who are outstanding examples of confidence:

1. _____
2. _____
3. _____
4. _____
5. _____

Why are they great examples for you?

_____
_____
_____

What could you learn from them?

_____
_____
_____
_____

WHAT BUILDS CONFIDENCE?

There are four areas in our lives that affect our confidence. They are:
1. Thinking
2. Skills
3. Relationships
4. Circumstances

The good news is that we have some degree of control over each of these areas. Our skills can be developed. The people we mix with can be chosen. We can direct our thinking, and many of the circumstances we find ourselves in are of our own design. So let's look at how your approach to each of these four areas can affect your confidence.

1. Thinking

Out thinking is all important. How we approach our skills, the way we relate to people, and how we respond to circumstances all depend on our thinking. Our attitudes and our beliefs are the most powerful forces in our world so let's look carefully at how we should shape them.

BELIEVE THAT SUCCESS IS OKAY

One of the foundation stones of great confidence is a positive view of success. Confidence requires subscription to the fact that it is possible and desirable to succeed. You cannot live confidently unless you believe in success! Success builds confidence and confidence breeds success. As strange as it may seem, many people are afraid of success. They may fear success in others or even fear their own.

The degree of success we are able to experience is prescribed by our own thinking. The first thing we need if we are to enjoy true success is a correct definition. The dictionary defines success as the attainment of something desired or intended, or the attainment of wealth or position.

It depends whose eyes you look through. Success in God's eyes is often very different from the way the world defines it.

I believe Godly success would be defined more like this: fruitfulness, influence outside your self, effectiveness outside your own world. It's more about who you are than what you've done. It's freedom to be who you were made to be. It's being who you were made to be and doing what you were made to do. It's enjoying life.

Notice I didn't mention money? Money is not success but a by-product of it. Sometimes money is the by-product of hard work, dishonesty, gambling, or illegal trade. Getting more stuff is not success either although a successful person may be able to access more stuff.

Jesus said, *"If you try to keep your life for yourself, you will lose it. But if you give up your life for me, you will find true life. And how do you benefit if you gain the whole world but lose or forfeit your own soul in the process?"*[2] Where is the success in getting all the stuff you want, only to end up leaving it all behind?

Godly success is never at the expense of anyone else - in fact part of true success is bringing success to others. We should determine to use whatever we have and whatever we acquire to the glory of God and to bless others.

Success is not a state you reach where you are problem-free, but a continuing journey of good decisions and wisdom that results in fruitfulness and effectiveness in your own world and outside it.

We need to understand that God wants us to succeed.[3] He designs it and He supports it. So what on God's green earth can hold us back from experiencing success? If it is God's will for us to be successful, nothing should be able to stop us… right? Wrong! We have free will and minds of our own. Our own thinking and actions can thwart the very plans of God if we allow them to. We derail many opportunities for success by acting out of our own small, negative and self-deprecating thinking.

A correct view of success provides a solid platform from which to launch our confidence. If we continually reinforce this balanced and healthy mindset our confidence will become wings on which to soar.

THE DIVINE VIEW

God's vision for us is one of incredible possibilities and brilliant success.
He sees us achieving at the highest level, succeeding extensively, being rewarded excessively, influencing the mighty!
He sees us undertaking impossible tasks, and completing them with courage.
He sees us marking people for life because of who we are - because of who He is in us.
He knows what we are capable of and sees us as we could be, not as we are;
*   Victorious over impossible odds,*
*   Standing firm though everything around us is shaken.*
*   Unstoppable, irrepressible, irresistible,*
*   Loyal, reliable, responsible, dependable,*
*   Generous, enthusiastic, bold, faith-filled, strong and courageous!*
He sees us being who we're made to be and doing what we were made to do.

What you become is far more important than what you get. What you get will be influenced by what you become.

JIM ROHN

Success is about who you are, not what you have. Successful people work to discover their talents, to develop those talents, and then to use those talents to benefit others as well as themselves.

TOM MORRIS

UNDERSTAND MY PURPOSE

If you have no sense of what you exist for it will be very difficult to approach life with enthusiasm and surety. Confidence requires a purpose to which it can attach itself. It needs a direction to which it can add impetus.

Knowing my calling is important here. If I know what God has placed in my hand to do I can go at it with boldness. On a large scale my purpose is "knowing God and making Him known", or to put it another way, "loving God and loving people to God". On a smaller scale it is "to lead Riverview Church into worship". If we bring the focus in tighter still, it is "to lead the Worship team." Then there are the particular tasks we do as a team. Confidence will come if I know what I'm trying to achieve and why.

KNOW WHAT GOD THINKS OF ME

The thoughts God has towards me are too numerous and too wonderful for me to know (Psalm 139). However, I do know some of them explicitly, and the nature of the rest of them. Here are a few:
> I exist because He wants me to, and I exist for Him (Romans 11:36)
> He planned my birth and designed me (Psalm 139)
> He loves me so much He died for me (John 3:16)
> He has good plans for my future (Jeremiah 29:11)
> … and so much more - and it's all good!

Start reciting the scriptures that declare what God thinks of you, and who you are in Christ. Write them out and use them as affirmations until they sink deep into your mind and become part of your thinking, until the first thoughts you have are the ones that reflect what God thinks. Making these truths part of your thinking will help you approach life confidently.

OPTIMISM

Positive thinking is a major key to confidence. You're not likely to walk onto a bridge if you think it's going to collapse when you're half-way across! Negative thinking produces nothing but discouragement and despondency, and will ensure that you never acquire confidence enough to have it destroyed.

Believe that life is good. Believe that God is good. Believe in people. Love life, love God, love people. Be an optimist and life will love you.

SUCCESSFUL SABOTAGE

Here are some of the ways we can sabotage our own success:

> *Not receiving compliments*
> *Not accepting gifts (including, "I don't accept charity")*
> *Not believing we deserve to have good "things"*
> *Not believing we deserve great circumstances or opportunities*
> *Not believing we deserve positions of influence*
> *Not believing God wants us to succeed*
> *Believing success will change us for the worse*
> *Thinking that one day it will just "happen" to us or for us*
> *Thinking that everyone should be equal, that no one has a right to have more or do better than another*
> *Fearing the response of others to our success. The Tall Poppy syndrome that cuts others down is the result of the fear that I will look bad if someone else does well.*
> *An "either/or" mentality. (i.e., if I'm successful, someone else will miss out)*

Is your confidence being inhibited by your view of success? Are there habits of action or thought that are holding you back? Scan through the list above and honestly evaluate whether you are sabotaging your success in any way. Write down what needs to change.

_____

_____

_____

_____

_____

_____

---

2. Skills

A number of factors in relation to our skills will enhance our confidence. (We will look at skill in more detail in the chapter Competence.)

COMPETENCE

Knowledge is power! There is nothing like "knowing your stuff". If you have put in the practice, if you've "done the work", your level of certainty is bound to rise.

You cannot consistently perform in a manner that is inconsistent with the way you see yourself.

JOHN MAXWELL

Confidence doesn't come out of nowhere. It's a result of something... hours and days and weeks and years of constant work and dedication.

ROGER STAUBACH

EXPERIENCE

When you have done it before, it's easy to believe you can do it again. If you've played a piece 99 times without making a mistake you can tackle it for the hundredth time with freedom and conviction.

WINS

They say, *"Nothing breeds success like success"*. If you have had a past success, your faith is built and you will find the confidence to attempt more difficult challenges. A sense of achievement and satisfaction comes from fulfilling even the smallest of goals. Creativity writer Julia Cameron advises, *"set gentle goals for yourself and reach them."* It sets you up for experiencing the feelings of success and that becomes a cycle. Small successes fuel your desire and your drive to achieve greater things.

PREPARATION

When you're well prepared, when you've planned well and practised well, you can move ahead with quiet assurance. You know you've positioned yourself for success.

CLEAR OBJECTIVES

It can be scary if you don't know where you're going. Inability to see is certain to make you tentative. It will always slow you down and cause you to hesitate even in the most trivial of pursuits. However, when you know exactly what you're supposed to do in a situation you can do it with confidence. If you're unsure - ask! Do all you can to put yourself in a position of certainty.

3. Relationships

Other people play a large role in the levels of our confidence. After all it is others for whom we work and perform. When it comes to key relationships, good choices are vital.

ENCOURAGEMENT

Some people have the ability to build your confidence while others can unwittingly tear it from you. Make sure you build relationships with supportive people. Choose to hang out with people who encourage you. For anything to grow, including confidence, it needs a nurturing environment.

ASSOCIATION

Business Philosopher, Jim Rohn, makes an important point: *"You must constantly ask yourself these questions: Who am I around? What are they doing to me? What have they got me reading? What have they got me* saying? Where do they have me going? What do they have me thinking? And most important, what do they have me becoming? Then ask yourself the big question: Is that okay?"

Proverbs 13:20 states, *"Whoever walks with the wise will become wise"*. The truth here is that we become like those with whom we associate. Confidence is contagious, and so is lack of confidence. So if you want to become more confident, hang out with more confident people! Look, listen and learn!

TEAM

As the Bible says, *"A person standing alone can be attacked and defeated, but two can stand back-to-back and conquer. Three are even better, for a triple-braided cord is not easily broken."[4]* Teaming with other confident people is powerful and can give you incredible confidence. The synergy of great partnership will help you feel unstoppable.

4. Circumstances

Some circumstances we have no control over. A marathon runner cannot choose the weather conditions for the day of his race. But he can influence many of the circumstances he finds himself in on that day. He can make sure that he arrives at the starting line with excellent running shoes and appropriate clothing. He can sleep well and prepare his body with a great training and nutrition schedule. He can set his alarm so he will have plenty of time to get emotionally prepared and arrive without having to rush… You get the picture. Making good choices in our everyday lives, and planning thoughtfully will set us up with circumstances that work for us rather than against us.

If you wait for perfect conditions, you will never get anything done.

Ecclesiastes 11:4 (NLT)

Circumstances are the rulers of the weak; they are but instruments of the wise.

Samuel Lover

SETTING UP FOR CONFIDENCE

Review the list of confidence builders and think about how you can incorporate them into your daily life. Are there any areas that could do with some extra attention right now?

Do I believe that success is okay?
Do I understand my purpose?
Do I know what God thinks of me?
Am I competent?
Do I have any wins under my belt?
Am I setting myself up for some small wins?
Do I prepare well?

Am I clear about what is expected of me and what I expect of myself?
Am I doing the right things to build adequate experience?
Do I approach life with optimism?
Have I formed relationships with encouraging people?
Am I associating with confident people?
Have I positioned myself in a team that brings support and strength?
Am I doing all I can to set up favourable circumstances for myself and for my endeavours?

Also, make the decision to be a person who builds confidence in other people.
How can I take what I've learned here and help others on their journey toward confidence?

WHAT DESTROYS CONFIDENCE?

Of course, if confidence can be built, it can be torn down. In fact, without a great foundation of good strong thinking, confidence is a puff of smoke that can dissolve in a moment. Let's look at some of the deadly enemies of confidence.

Inhibitions

I find water very soothing and relaxing so I took some time out to sit beside the river one day and rest. As I was looking out across the river I saw a dog running around excitedly, jumping into the shallow water and frisking around. He was so carefree, enjoying God's creation with vigour. I wondered why we humans don't do that. I know children can, but with every year we seem to lose a little more of that total freedom.

We are born confident. Yet, as we grow we become aware of failure to meet expectations - our own and those of others. We become self-conscious and begin to develop inhibitions. We gain responsibilities, and our range and degree of inhibitions grow. These erode our confidence or, in other words, they inhibit our ability to operate with confidence.

Some inhibitions are necessary and appropriate but many are not. To shine as we were created to we need to rise above these inhibitions.

Many inhibitions come from a fear of what others may think about us. We are concerned that we may not please them or impress them. Rather than face the pain of being rejected we develop "safe" behaviour, and so we are inhibited, no longer free to express ourselves fully.

Sometimes the pressure to please others interferes with our ability to do what we were created, designed, called and anointed to do. If something is interfering with what we were made for, then it is inhibiting our ability to live fully for God. We need to sort through our inhibitions and find which ones are necessary to please God, and which ones are there purely to protect us from the rejection or disapproval of others.

BOLD AS BRASS
an exercise in challenging inhibitions

If it wasn't so embarrassing, I'd:

1. _____
2. _____
3. _____
4. _____
5. _____

If I knew without a doubt everyone would support me, I'd:

1. _____
2. _____
3. _____
4. _____
5. _____

CREATIVITY AND FEAR

Fear is the opposite of confidence. It cripples our ability to create and make great art. In fact, fear impedes our ability to do anything well. It destroys our confidence and incapacitates us, snuffing out our light.

There are many fears we could have in the process of being creative or using our particular talents, and numerous reasons for these fears. Here are some of the fears and thinking flaws that will undermine confidence:

Comparison

This is when we measure ourselves against others - thinking that if they perform better than we do, we're no good. This fear comes from attaching our self-worth to what we do.

Jazz musician, Kenny Werner, has observed it this way: *"It seems as if in order to be good you have to play good. Musicians who fall into this trap generally don't enjoy life. Every day brings anxiety. They are either elated or depressed. Each solo is the acid test of apparent worth. Their self-respect is as volatile as the stock market. They rarely play anything of depth. They are like the person who is always trying to get us to like him; we usually don't."*[5]

We have to have a reason for living that is greater than what we do. In the team I lead - Riverview Worship Team - we have a purpose that is more important than the singing and the music. It is "to purposefully lead people into the presence of God." We're there to help others express worship, not to show how good we are at expressing ourselves. When we get our eyes off ourselves and on our purpose together, how we compare to the person next to us is put in perspective.

Tall Poppy Syndrome

We may be afraid of being outstanding, or being a "tall poppy." We may think that by doing well we'll upset others and somehow ruin their chances of success.

Marianne Williamson gives a stunning rebuttal: *"We ask ourselves, who am I to be brilliant, gorgeous, talented and fabulous? Actually, who are you not to be? You are a child of God. Your playing small doesn't serve the world. There's nothing enlightened about shrinking so that other people won't feel insecure around you. We were born to make manifest the glory of God that is within us. It's not just in some of us; it's in everyone. And as we let our own light shine, we unconsciously give other people permission to do the same. As we're liberated from our fear, our presence automatically liberates others."*[6]

There is no virtue in holding back for the sake of others because they may feel threatened or jealous. Such people may never be satisfied and it is not your duty to tip-toe around their insecurities.

Some people have the notion that we are all equal and no one should stand out. They are completely mistaken. The Bible very clearly states that each person has different gifts; we are all unique. Obviously, some are going to be more natural and more skilled than others when they are working in the area of their gifting. This is a good thing.

Using your gift in a God-honouring way will inspire people, not threaten them. Be confident of what God has called you to and don't allow the insecurities of others to bully you off the path.

Scarcity Mindset

Our materialistic world-view tells us that the world is only so big. Resources are limited. There's only so much to go around. It's like a pie and if I get a bigger piece, someone else must get a smaller one.

We are forgetting that God created the world - "out of nothing"! Who is the source of all creativity? Is He going to run out? There is not a limited amount of creativity to go around. Imagination knows no bounds! An abundance mindset will bolster your confidence. Always tell yourself, "There's more where that came from!"

Fear of Exposing Yourself

Art-making is very personal. An artist's work is a window to his soul. Showing who we really are - wearing our heart on our sleeve, pulling back the curtains on our inner world - can be very scary. Artist, Anne Truitt, in her published journal Daybook says that artists must *"spin their work out of themselves, discover its law, and then present themselves turned inside out to the public gaze."*

Unveiling our work is a risk because people may not accept or understand it. And even if they do accept or understand it, they may not like it. We can then feel rejected personally because what we create comes right from the heart of us.

The irony is that our art is most persuasive, passionate and impacting when we bare our souls. There's something in its vulnerability that connects with people. It has emotional resonance. It carries the weight of credibility.

Our creative gifts are meant to be displayed, so we must learn to be comfortable expressing them openly. Knowing that we have worth as a person - even before we've begun to create - will help us to be free in expression.

You can't use up creativity. The more you use, the more you have.

Maya Angelou, poet

Be who you are and say what you feel, because those who mind don't matter and those who matter don't mind.

Dr. Suess

Self-Expectation

We may worry that we won't come up to our own high expectations. We are constantly measuring ourselves against what we know we are capable of - our personal best. The fact is that it is totally unrealistic to expect to achieve personal bests every time we perform. Remember, out of a thousand performances, only one can be our personal best.

We must not allow the fear of not performing at full potential paralyse us. *"A person who is not afraid to die, knows how to live. A person who is not afraid to fail, succeeds. And a person who is not afraid to sound terrible may sound great. It isn't guaranteed, because there are other factors involved - but this essential element must be there."*[7]

At the Sydney 2000 Olympic Games, Maurice Green from the USA won the gold medal in the 100m. He didn't set a new world record. He didn't even set a personal best. But 100,000 people in the stadium stood and cheered, and millions watching by television were mesmerised as in 10 short seconds Maurice did what he was made to do. There's no doubt that millions were inspired by that performance! I'm pretty sure that he would have thought it acceptable too!

Be realistic about the results you expect from yourself. Be kind to yourself. Allow for cycles in your performance.

Others' Expectations

Often we're concerned that we won't fulfil the high expectations of others. We become overly self-conscious. We have the false belief that others would expect even more from us than we do from ourselves.

Writer William Saroyan's insight is encouraging: *"All writers are discontented with their work as it's being made. That's because they are always aware of a potential, and believe they're not reaching it. But the reader is not aware of the potential so it makes no difference to him."*

Imagination begins in the mind of the performer but finishes in the mind of the beholder. This is true for the musician, artist, writer or any kind of creator. This is an incredibly freeing truth once we can accept it.

Some years ago now, when I was starting out with recording, I didn't understand this principle. I would be trying to nail a guitar solo and I'd want to do it again… and again… and again… until it drove everyone crazy. I would never be happy with what I'd done, even after numerous takes. They would say it was great, but I couldn't be convinced. What I was suffering from was measuring my actual performance against the "perfect solo" in my head. Of course, it never measured up.

It took a few years, but I finally learned to trust the judgement of those around me. They actually want me to succeed just as much as I do. If they say it's great - it is great!

As Philip Toshio Sudo instructs, *"Do not beat up on yourself. Even if you think you know your flaws, there is no need to advertise them. Most people wouldn't have noticed."*

IMPERFECTLY OK
an exercise in challenging perfectionism

If I didn't have to do it perfectly, I would:

1. _____
2. _____
3. _____
4. _____
5. _____

The "I'm a pretender" Fear

This one certainly plagued me for a while. As a musician I had been self-taught for twenty years and played only "by ear". I always felt insecure around musicians who I knew had strong musical backgrounds. I overcame this insecurity by devoting two years to a formal music education, discovering along the way the background and theory to what was already part of my playing.

An information vacuum will always produce uncertainty. Confidence is always built on knowledge - knowledge of something, or knowledge of someone. Likewise, not many thrive on walking into new or overwhelming circumstances without adequate preparation. For most of us the unknown is terrifying! So the antidote to this particular fear is education. Get more information, get training, and learn as much as you can about your area of interest.

Unoriginal

Some of us are afraid to put our shoulder to the wheel for fear that we won't be totally original. What if we produce something that's already been done?

It is merely an irrational demand of our ego to produce totally original work. Irrational because none of us could ever legitimately lay claim to being 100 percent original. We are all influenced by the people with whom we associate, and by what we see and hear around us, from billboards to television, radio to movies. All work is influenced by other work.

As the poet John Donne said, *"no man is an island"*. It is equally true for art and industry - there is no piece of work that doesn't have roots in another.

Possibility Paralysis

Fear of cutting off or closing down alternatives can paralyse our progress, or even prevent us from beginning. We may be afraid of choosing a certain path - what if another would have ended up giving a better result?

Once you commit to going in a certain direction, your flexibility is reduced. The options thin out. But that is the price of progress. Completing a work actually requires the disciplined and unrelenting cutting away of alternative possibilities until you're left with just the one possibility.

The root of this creativity block is perfectionism. We must remind ourselves that "perfect" work is the fantasy of an idealistic mind. When we understand that it's okay simply to do our best, we will be able to make the creative decisions and move ahead.

"I'm past it! I've lost the touch!"

Many of us, including myself, fear that our best work has been done. Creativity and inspiration can be quite a mystery. We can't always put our finger on how a piece of work finds its way from the spark of an idea to become a glorious entity that seems to have its own "life". It takes faith to believe it can all happen again.

Here are some keys to defusing the power of this fear:
> Know God's plan is for a good future. That has to include the on-going effective use of your gifts. Cultivate hope in your life by reminding yourself that God is your partner in this.

To require perfection is to invite paralysis.

David Bayles and Ted Orland

The poem in the head is always perfect. Resistance begins when you try to convert it into language.

Stanley Kunitz

> Take the mystery out of creativity by making it a daily practice. Do the work whether you feel inspired or not. Those who take this approach will always end up producing work in greater quantity as well as finer quality.

> Have a big-picture view of your work. Try and see a lifetime body of work and understand that there will be a progression of maturity punctuated by highlights along the way. Some of your work, indeed most of it, will be ordinary. It's all important to the journey, and those works that stand out owe their existence to the lessons learnt and skills gained while doing ordinary work.

There are many "one hit wonders" in the history of music, art, invention and industry. However, if we take a closer look we will inevitably find that the standout "hit" does not stand alone, but as an integral part of a lifetime body of work.

"It's too late! I'm too old!"

Another fear is that we've "missed the boat" when it comes to discovering our calling and living creatively. We look at the time passed and see it as wasted, rather than looking to the future and the time we still have.

When I finally took the plunge and went to music college, I was at least 10 years older than most of my classmates. However, I was also much hungrier to learn. I had more life experience, and was far more intentional than most of them. As a result I did better than most. As they say, it's never too late to start. You're not too old until you're dead! (There was a lady in one of my classes who was over 60 - that's inspirational!)

I CAN!

recognising and overcoming fears

Skim through the above "creativity fears" and ask yourself which ones you have struggled with.

_____

_____

_____

It is never too late to be what you might have been.

GEORGE ELIOT

There are a lot of things we don't have in life, but time is not one of them. Time is all we have. One lifetime under this name to produce a body of work that says, 'This is how I saw the world.' Your work is worthy of whatever time it takes.

JAN PHILLIPS

What can you do to overcome these fears and build your confidence?

_____

_____

_____

_____

Where will you begin?

_____

_____

_____

_____

Building confidence is like building anything. It requires consistent attention and effort. Our goal should be to build habits in our lives that develop our skills. We also need to cultivate habits that bring us into regular contact with positive and inspiring people, and habits that will feed our minds and cause us to think constructively. If we are diligent with these steps there is no doubt we will be rewarded with steadily growing confidence.

PART TWO
living out loud:
putting confidence to work

CHARISMA

I remember seeing U2 on their "Love Town" Tour in the early 1990's. It was an amazing show, but what struck me most was the incredible presence Bono brought with him the moment he stepped onto the stage. He appeared supremely confident and totally at ease with his position of power, enjoying having a stadium of 20,000 people in his hands.

Some people, like Bono, seem to be naturally charismatic. They ooze personality and have the effortless ability to engage people. They have something about them that's attractive and makes people want to be around them. Their appealing personality causes others to respond to them.

Much of this great quality is due to confidence. Someone at ease with herself finds it easy to be at ease with others. Because she is at ease with others, they in turn are at ease with her. She makes them feel good about themselves and their confidence rises.

Charisma is a quality that can be developed, just as confidence can. It is all about relating to others. This personal magnetism doesn't appear out of thin air, but is usually the result of a generous spirit. Someone who inspires, encourages, cares about, motivates and is interested in others will also win their hearts. If we always strive to make people feel comfortable and valuable we will win friends and influence people.

BOLDNESS

Boldness is pro-active and takes confidence to new levels. The bold take themselves to the challenge before the challenge comes to them! To be bold is to be brave, daring, imaginative, innovative, conspicuous, and full of faith. Bold people are not timid or tentative and are willing to take a risk.

Bold people are inspiring. They stir our hearts and emotions because they pursue ideals and dreams that most of us would love to pursue - if only we had the courage.

Part of my dream is to see a vibrant, passionate worshipping church - one that is free and uncontained in its expression of love to God. Another part is to see vibrant, passionate and confident musicians, singers and creative artists in the community of faith. I so intensely want to help people find freedom in their calling, creativity and expression. I'm crazy enough to give my life to this. I'm living boldly in pursuit of this goal!

You have to be bold to dream big dreams. Darlene Zschech's dream is to make a difference in the way people worship in every church on the planet! THAT is a big dream! Here's what she said:

> One of the things that I wrote down as part of my dream, is that I will have a major part to play in changing not only the face, but the heart of every worshipper in every church on the planet. That I will have a major part to play in training up the greatest worship teams ever, the greatest songwriters that have ever graced Heaven with a song. Teams that have a revelation of the power of praise and worship. That God's army of worshippers will no longer struggle with the call of God on their lives, but will stand strong in His purpose. I want to have a part to play in changing hearts, pointing people to Christ with every step they take, every breath they breathe. That's just a little bit of my dream...[8]

History shows that it's those who have been bold enough to dream big dreams who have impacted the world.

Why Be Bold?

You need to be bold to think big, to dream big, to be generous, to speak life into other people's worlds. You've got to be bold to get outside of your comfort zone and push the limits in your own life. You need boldness to try things you've never done before, to be creative, to go beyond the normal.

You need boldness to be an extravagant worshipper! There's a certain Godly recklessness, a passion that denies self-consciousness required to go there.

Being bold is having a faith approach to life. An optimistic, positive, believing approach. One that speaks well of your future. One that reaches out for the glory of what could be. One that draws the impossible right into its grasp!

Growing in Boldness

Here are six ways to develop your boldness;

1. KNOW WHAT YOU BELIEVE
When you know that you know that you know, it's easy to be bold! Boldness is born of conviction. Know what you believe, be sure of it, be persuaded of its truth - this will give you the courage to walk and talk it.

2. HAVE A VISION
You need to know what you want. What do you want to see or achieve? There's no motivation like wanting something desperately. It will make you bold enough to go after it!

I bought my first "real" professional guitar amp set up in 1989 with a $5,500 bank loan! I had nothing else in the way of possessions at the time - no car, no fridge, no bed. Just some clothes and a guitar. I made that bold move because I knew what I wanted. I could 'see' my future!

When you can see what you want you'll be passionate and passion will make you bold. A vision of what can be will motivate you and bring bold action out of you.

3. GET AROUND BOLD PEOPLE
As I said earlier, bold people inspire us. They stir up the dreams within us and make the impossible seem possible. We need to mix with people of faith, action and excellence as often as possible. As the Bible says, *"Become wise by walking with the wise."*[9] We become like those with whom we associate.

4. LEARN TO ENJOY GETTING OUTSIDE YOUR COMFORT ZONE
It's always a risk to be bold. If there is nothing to lose, then boldness isn't required. It's not needed to do easy things. However, it is needed to stand out from the pack, to pursue excellence, and to speak up for the best when everyone is happy with good.

Any time we say Let there be! In any form, something happens!

Stella Terrill Mann

Confidence awakens confidence.

Friedrich Von Sachsen

For many of us, meeting new people or making new friends is fraught with anxiety. Boldness is required. We need to ignore the fear of rejection, the "what if they don't like me?" voices, believing rather that the possibility of gaining a genuine friendship, someone to share the richness of life with, is well worth the risk.

5. UNDERSTAND THE RESULTS OF YOUR BOLDNESS
Your boldness will affect your world profoundly. It will also affect everyone around you. It enlarges your world and theirs.

Boldness brings freedom. It refuses to submit to inhibition. It refuses to be contained by old boundaries and so breaks new ground. Boldness brings breakthrough.

When we're bold, opportunity is released. I remember when I was told that Riverview Church was looking for a Music Director. Within a couple of days I had a strong sense that this was an opportunity God had put before me. I remember being very bold in pursuing this position, even though I had no experience as a Music Director in any church, let alone a large church. I pushed hard on the doors of opportunity and they opened before me. Boldness allows you to take the initiative. It knows that "nothing ventured equals nothing gained".

Boldness releases favour. It takes fortitude to ask! *"And yet the reason you don't have what you want is that you don't ask God for it."*[10] As John Dryden observed, *"Fortune befriends the bold."* When a Gentile woman asks Jesus to heal her child, his answer insinuates that she is a dog. Her bold reply - *"even dogs get the crumbs!"* Jesus is impressed at her faith and audacity and grants her request.[11]

Boldness brings faith. It chooses to look beyond the obstacles and the "facts" to see potential and possibilities. It knows faith is more powerful than fear. It is prepared to "feel the fear and do it anyway."

Boldness is an important mark of leadership - you can lead without it, but if you add boldness to your leadership it will be far more effective. It inspires others to step out. Consider how inspired Peter was when he saw Jesus walking on the water!

6. KNOW WHO YOU ARE
Make sure you know who God says you are. When you know who made you and why, you can be full of confidence. You can be bold because you know who is backing you. If He is for you who can be against you?

Boldness grows out of confidence - not self-confidence but God-confidence or faith. You must believe that He has given you something and it has significance and worth.

When you know your gifts and your strengths, and you know your areas of weakness, you can press ahead with assurance. Add to this an understanding of your godly calling and you can step out knowing you're doing the right thing and you're in the right place.

Dream big dreams. Take bold action. LIVE A BOLD LIFE!!!

FAITH

Faith is another aspect of confidence. Faith is the kind of confidence that can "see" the future. It sees a future that is bigger, better and brighter. It believes in what it can "see" even though it does not yet exist.

Many of us are afraid of the unknown; we need faith to walk into the future without hesitation.

A faith-filled person is a confident person. Faith takes a positive approach to the unknown. Faith is facing the future with optimism even when we don't know all the details and dangers. Faith is necessary when things are beyond our control. Of course, much of life is this way. We can't control the weather, or other people's driving habits, or the wheels on a supermarket trolley, or the price of fish!

However, faith is more than optimism. We place our faith in something or someone, knowing that they can be depended on. Of course, as a Christian we can count on God because we know He is good, He is merciful and He has great plans for our future. Our faith is based on the immutably good and infinitely dependable character of God.

If you don't risk anything, you risk even more.

Erica Jong

Expectation is the breeding ground of the miraculous.

Darlene Zschech

PULLING WEEDS
an exercise in changing thought patterns

Seeds of doubt grow into unbelief and lack of confidence. Seeds of pain or ridicule grow into towering fears. With this in mind, let's forage through the undergrowth of our thinking and discover which plants are legitimate and helpful, and which need to be removed and replaced.

Here are five thoughts or beliefs I hold that could inhibit my ability to live confidently: *(Example: "I'm just not good with money", or, "my memory is terrible")*

1. _____
2. _____
3. _____
4. _____
5. _____

Think about what thoughts you could use as antidotes to these and create positive affirmations to combat them.
(Example: "I'm becoming financially astute. I'm learning about money and how to handle it and am building my confidence and security day by day.")

1. _____
2. _____
3. _____
4. _____
5. _____

prayer

Faithful and dependable God, I know I can have complete confidence in You. Help me to live as if I believe it. I want to represent You with persuasive conviction. I want to be who You made me to be and live a bold life, bringing hope and life to others. Help me never to be arrogant but to be unshakably secure in who I am. I love You! Amen.

contract

Commitment to Confidence

I, _____, am committed to growing in confidence. I will work at changing my thinking where it needs to be changed. I will take steps and make choices that will set me up for success. I am going to ensure I know what I believe about God, about me and about life. I am going to build friendships with positive and encouraging people.

Signature _____ Date _____

ENDNOTES

1. Joshua 1:6-9
2. Luke 9:24-25
3. Jeremiah 29:11 "For I know the plans I have for you," says the LORD. "They are plans for good and not for disaster, to give you a future and a hope."
   John 10:10 "The thief's purpose is to steal and kill and destroy. My purpose is to give life in all its fullness."
   1 Corinthians 2:9 However, as it is written: "No eye has seen, no ear has heard, no mind has conceived what God has prepared for those who love him."
   Deuteronomy 8:18 "Always remember that it is the LORD your God who gives you power to become rich, and he does it to fulfil the covenant he made with your ancestors."
4. Ecclesiastes 4:12
5. Werner, Kenny: *Effortless Mastery*; Jamey Aebersold Jazz, Inc., New Albany, IN; www.jajazz.com; 1996, p30.
6. Williamson, Marianne: *A Return To Love: Reflections on the Principles of A Course in Miracles*, Harper Collins, 1992, (from Chapter 7, Section 3)
7. Werner, Kenny: ibid p39.
8. Zschech, Darlene: *Extravagant Worship*, Check Music Ministries, Castle Hill, Australia; 2001, p197.
9. Proverbs 13:20 *The Message*
10. James 4:2
11. Mark 7:24-30

competence
a performance that shines

competence

To describe someone as competent would suggest that he or she has the required qualities or adequate ability; is legally qualified; or, has the capacity to function or develop in a particular way. We would expect that person is proficient, adept, knowledgeable and skilled. Simply put, he or she has what it takes to get the job done well.

Great character and a great attitude are wonderful and necessary, but they are not enough. Add passion and you have a potent mix, but it's still not enough. You must have a certain level of proficiency to be truly effective. Without competence you'll be running around in circles achieving very little and inspiring no one.

THE CASE FOR COMPETENCE

There is a lengthy passage in the book of Exodus concerning the crafting of objects to be used in worship in the Tabernacle. If you skim through chapters 26 - 39, you will notice over and over the words skill, skilled and skilfully. They are applied to all kinds of craftsmen, from tailors and gemstone experts to metal workers, incense makers and embroiderers. Clearly, God wanted competent craftsmen and artisans working on His projects.

When David restored the Ark of the Covenant to Jerusalem and when Solomon built the Temple, they knew God required the best in all things. Throughout 1 and 2 Chronicles we find mention of training, skill, expertise and accomplishment.[1] Competence in the house of God was taken seriously, just as it should be today.

As creative people, one of our greatest goals is to communicate well through our creativity. It's essential, then, that we develop our technique to the point where it doesn't inhibit our expression - where it doesn't hold us back from saying what we want to say and making the point we want to make; where we can evoke the emotional responses we intend.

Competence is not static; it can increase or decrease. The good news is that each of us can improve our skills and increase our knowledge. The bad news is the bar is continually rising. Information, methods and technology are constantly advancing, continually presenting us with the threat of being "left behind". Competence can be ours if we will combine a little bit of talent with a lot of discipline, effort and experience.

Competence is invaluable to leadership and influence. A polished performance communicates well and inspires people. Someone who is able to execute tasks with expertise builds credibility and breeds confidence.

Competence can take you places in life that nothing else can. In the Old Testament, the book of Daniel tells the story of an incredible young man. Daniel *"soon proved himself more capable than all the other administrators and princes. Because of his great ability, the king made plans to place him over the entire empire."*[2] If we are to shine in the darkness with maximum luminosity, competence is essential.

The most compelling force on the planet is an outstanding example.

MARK CULLEN

Commitment and talent are unconnected - unless you connect them.

JOHN MAXWELL

EXPANDING ABILITIES
committing to competence

What are my three main areas of expertise?

1. _____

2. _____

3. _____

On a scale of one to ten, how would I rate my current level of competence in these areas?

1. *Poor*   *1 2 3 4 5 6 7 8 9 10*   *Outstanding*
2. *Poor*   *1 2 3 4 5 6 7 8 9 10*   *Outstanding*
3. *Poor*   *1 2 3 4 5 6 7 8 9 10*   *Outstanding*

What have I done most recently to enhance and polish these skills?

_____

_____

_____

_____

_____

What steps could I take to polish these gems of ability further and improve their shine?

1. _____

2. _____

3. _____

4. _____

5. _____

6. _____

Which of these steps will I take and when?

_____

_____

_____

_____

The king is the man who can.

THOMAS CARLYLE

Ability will never catch up with the demand for it.

MALCOLM S. FORBES

EXCELLENCE

It is true that success will not be attained without competence, but those who shine go much further than simply qualifying or having adequate skill. Shiners excel. Their focus is on excellence and exceeding expectations, not merely meeting requirements or fulfilling obligations. We need to learn to value excellence.

To excel is to surpass expectations; be more or greater than normal; go beyond the usual; be immoderate; or, be above average. Wouldn't you like that sentence to describe your life?

There is no doubt that Daniel stood out from the rest. When *"the other administrators and princes began searching for some fault in the way*

Daniel was handling his affairs… they couldn't find anything to criticize. He was faithful and honest and always responsible."[3] Excellence sets one apart from the average. A commitment to a life less ordinary will ensure there is bright-burning oil in your lamp.

Excellence doesn't just happen. It requires focus, attention and dedication. Most often it is a journey of many small steps of intentional improvement. It takes concentration and diligent effort but these produce impressive results.

Why Pursue Excellence?

In his book Rediscovering Church, Pastor Bill Hybels outlines the values on which Willow Creek Community Church has been built. One of the values this large and thriving church holds is that *Excellence honours God and inspires people.* If this is true then it follows that the pursuit of excellence is an honourable pursuit.

Honouring God

The Apostle Paul urges us, *"Whatever you do, work at it with all your heart, as working for the Lord, not for men."[4]* He's saying, go to the limits of your effort, do your very best and do it with a great attitude. In another letter he tells us that *"your everyday, ordinary life - your sleeping, eating, going-to-work, and walking-around life,"[5]* is how your worship to God is packaged. Our whole approach to life will define the quality of our worship to Him. What we give to God should be the best - not the dregs or the scraps left over at the end. Excellence honours God.

Another angle here is that we represent God to others. We are created by God, in His image, and as such, whatever we do reflects on Him. When we value and display excellence we represent Him well and bring honour to His name.

Inspiring People

Excellence doesn't distract from our purpose; it makes it clearer and enhances people's experience. There is no doubt that people are inspired by superior performances and by achievements that have been expertly conceived and completed. We humans have an innate attraction to that which is wonderful. The exquisite and the grand capture our attention, I think, because they whisper of the origin of all splendour, greatness and goodness. They point towards the Perfect.

THE ARGUMENT FOR IGNORANCE

Some who have been blessed with talent are afraid to study formally or learn too much about their particular field of giftedness. They fear that somehow the "magic" will disappear and they'll lose their natural abilities, the mystery will evaporate and all they'll be left with is a handful of smoke.

Nobel prize-winning physicist, Richard Feynman, challenged this mindset:

Poets say science takes away from the beauty of the stars - mere globs of gas atoms. I too can see the stars on a desert night, and feel them. But do I see less or more? The vastness of the heavens stretches my imagination - stuck on this carousel my little eye can catch one-million-year-old light. A vast pattern - of which I am a part... What is the pattern, or the meaning, or the why? It does not do harm to the mystery to know a little about it. For far more marvelous is the truth than any artists of the past imagined it. Why do the poets of the present not speak of it? What men are poets who can speak of Jupiter if he were a man, but if he is an immense spinning sphere of methane and ammonia must be silent.[6]

Learning from others and having influences cannot ruin your uniqueness unless you go overboard. Growing can only enhance it. Steve Vai is a virtuoso rock guitarist. In response to the comment that "A lot of rock musicians would rather not learn to read music or know theory," Vai says:

"For me, I like to know the music because it helps my expression. I can sit with manuscript paper and compose music that I couldn't do if I didn't know music. The big mistake some people make is thinking that if you know music you can't play from the heart, but it's all up to the individual. Those statements usually come from someone who hasn't taken the time or had the discipline to sit and learn. If they did, they'd realize that there's a whole other world of expression."[7]

Cultivating Excellence

Excellence requires attention to detail. It means getting the basics and the small things right. Quality is always proven in the details.

Excellence also requires awareness of the big picture. The details are always found within the context of a bigger picture. If we are to excel we need to pay attention to the whole setting. For example, in the worship team in our Church, most of our details are concentrated within the first twenty to thirty minutes of the service. However, to really display excellence we need to be committed to the success of the whole service.

When you give your best to the world, the world returns the favour.

H. Jackson Brown

Excellence is no accident.

Phil Pringle

The big picture includes the fact that people are looking to us for leadership before, during and after the service. How we take part in the rest of the service matters.

Excellence doesn't look for short cuts - it goes the second mile. Statements like, "Oh, that'll do", "Near enough is good enough", "It'll be all right on the night", "We'll fix it in the mix", or asking, "Will this do?" are indicators that we are not committed to excellence. We need to have the attitude that says, "Only my best will do", not, "What can I get away with?"

Excellence will only materialise in the measure that we are willing to pay for it. Henry Ward Beecher gave us this valuable advice: "*Hold yourself responsible for a higher standard than anybody expects of you. Never excuse yourself.*" Start earlier, stay longer, go faster and focus more intensely. Do more and do it with greater attention to quality than is required. That is the way of excellence.

Excellence must be valued. Great art and significant creative achievement can only be the product of a community or environment where excellence is highly regarded. Excellence shows up where it is valued. My Senior Pastor, Philip Baker, states it in reverse, *"The kind of thinking that puts up with the shabby, sloppy, wishy-washy, mediocre and insipid, rings the death-knell on achievement, innovation and creativity every time."*[8]

Excellence requires consistency. You don't get a reputation for excellence by occasionally getting it right! The famous former NFL coach, Vince Lombardi, said, *"You don't do things right once in a while, you do them right all the time."* This is the approach that brought Lombardi a reputation as an excellent coach.

Of course, excellence begins with our minds. The Apostle Paul gives us a perfect prescription for the cultivation of an excellent thought life. *"Fix your thoughts on what is true and honourable and right. Think about things that are pure and lovely and admirable. Think about things that are excellent and worthy of praise."*[9]

Take The High Road

A spirit of excellence will pervade and improve every part of our lives. It will result in an exemplary lifestyle, illuminating the path for others. It will affect our work, our relationships and our attitudes.

Pat Riley said, *"Excellence is the gradual result of always striving to do better."* The pursuit of excellence is a continuing journey and we must take it. We must not pull up on the side of the road at a place we consider excellent, since what is excellent today may well be average in a year's time. It is, however, a very fulfilling and rewarding journey. You, and everyone around you, will be glad you're taking it.

HELPFUL HABITS
an exercise in cultivating excellence

Do I hold excellence as a value in my life?

Which of my habits prove this?

What new habits should I cultivate to uphold my commitment to excellence?

Over the next month I will develop the habit of

OUTSTANDING EXAMPLES

I am convinced that the most compelling force on the planet is an outstanding example. This is a person who is competent, and committed to excellence in what they do and who they are. On their journey they have grappled with their gift and mixed discipline with desire, steadily growing in capability and confidence.

What kind of player, performer, communicator or athlete do you find inspirational? The beginner, the busker, the jack-of-all-trades-master-of-none, or the one whose every note, line or step is filled with conviction, control and grace, and is able to move you to your core?

Remember the proverb that says, *"Do you see a man skilled in his work? He will stand before kings; He will not stand before obscure men."*[10] We would all rather be working for kings and rulers, but these stations are reserved for those who are outstanding. Those who secure positions of responsibility, esteem and influence, are those who have mastered not only their skills, but also themselves.

When we see an artist or sportsperson, or anyone for that matter, succeeding, we are seeing only the "tip of the iceberg". (Only 10% of an iceberg is visible above the waterline.) We are seeing the adulation, the influence, the polished performance. What we don't see are the years, the tears and the fears that have shaped their whole life. These formative experiences have produced an environment in which their gifts and skills can emerge and flourish.

It's very easy to believe in "overnight success" because that is how we actually see it most of the time. Successful people are unknown to us until they "make it". Our perception is that they've just begun, when in fact, they have lived 20 or 30 years working towards what they have just achieved.

It's easy to watch someone being successful and think we'd like to do what they do and do it as well, thinking that maybe in six months or a year we could achieve it. Immature artists watch others and say competitively and egotistically, "I can do that!" Mature artists watch admiringly and think, "I could do that", possessing a little more understanding about the obstacles on the road and the length of the journey it would take to get there.

I think most of the time only the person concerned, and God, truly know what they've been through to get where they are. But there are some common threads that run through the lives of those who stand out from the rest.

There are no half-hearted champions.

JOHN MAXWELL

The difference between "average" people and "great" people can be summed up in three words: "And then some."

JAMES E. BYRNES

ALL-OUT HEALTH
maximising your potential to perform

Obviously, to achieve the highest levels of competence - to operate masterfully, we need to be in fine form physically, emotionally and spiritually.

If we fail to keep healthy in these areas and can't perform at our peak, we sabotage our own success. We need to be physically fit, emotionally sound and spiritually vital. Looking after ourselves is essential if we are to live long-lasting, bright-burning lives.

Do I see my holistic health as a high priority?

_____

_____

_____

Is there a lack of condition in any area that is impeding my performance?

_____

_____

_____

What habits could I change (or develop) that would improve my spiritual, emotional or physical health and potentially impact my competence?

_____

_____

_____

_____

There is no path to success, you make one by taking the first step!

UNKNOWN

Spectacular achievements come from unspectacular preparation.

ROGER STAUBACH

Seven Common Traits of Prominent Artists and Outstanding Examples:

1. PASSION
Those who are at the pinnacle of their profession are people who love what they do - they're fully into it! Their eyes light up and they come to life when they come across someone else who shares their passion. They have a hunger to learn, and a deep desire to develop in this area.

2. PREOCCUPATION

People who exceed the average devote unreasonable amounts of time and thought to their area of giftedness. I say unreasonable because others would often view them as fanatical or unbalanced. Because it is a major priority in their life, they focus nearly all their energy into this area and the results show. *"Mozart worked prodigiously hard at his chosen area of creative expression. It is reported that he would often work as many as 18 hours a day."*[11] Likewise, Johann Sebastian Bach habitually worked 10 - 18 hours a day for almost 60 years.

3. PROACTIVE

Outstanding examples understand that their destiny is in their hands. They realise that they must do something. They believe that they are in the driver's seat of their life. They believe in choice over chance. They don't wait for it to happen magically but take the initiative to search out opportunity and find ways to put themselves in its path. They actively seek out ways to improve and develop - finding experienced mentors, getting lessons, buying books, magazines and other resources.

4. PRACTICE

Prominent artists practise! They stimulate consistent growth by stretching and reinforcing their skills. They know that skill is developed and strengthened through repetition and thoroughness and they don't expect it to be exciting. They strengthen their skill by coming at it from many different angles. Each approach enhances their understanding.

What does it take to perform at the pinnacle of competition - the Olympic Games or the World Championships? Studies indicate that on average it takes 10,000 hours of practice to develop a world-class athlete (to do that you'd need to practice 4hrs a day for nearly 7 years!)

5. PATIENCE AND PERSEVERANCE

One of the keys to prodigious performance is to understand the power of process.

The analogy of growing plants is helpful once again. You prepare the best soil, then plant the seeds and water them. You provide the best possible conditions. You can't come back the next day and expect to harvest juicy ripe fruit! You can only do your part, then time and seasons and experience all play their part. Skills and talent work the same way. We do all we can then time, trials and experience do their work. We must be patient and believe success is in process.

We must think: I know that God has a plan for me, and that it is a good plan, one that gives me a future. I am not hoping in vain - there is an end point to this particular journey, and it's God's will that I reach it.[12] If we have faith like this it will help us to be disciplined, determined, tenacious and hard working.

Joshua had to be very patient. For him the Promised Land was 40 years away - but it was definitely coming. There was never any other ending in God's mind. Thomas Edison's persistence is legendary. He performed over 9,000 experiments to perfect the incandescent light bulb, and more than 50,000 to invent the storage-cell battery!

6. PAY THE PRICE

Those who outshine the rest know that to be outstanding costs a lot, but they're willing to pay - in fact they're big spenders! They will spend large portions of time and copious amounts of effort. They spend money on their passion as if nothing else matters. They are prepared to sacrifice other pleasures and delights too.

When I was a teenager, I could have gotten hooked on snow skiing or surfing but I chose to spend my money and time on music and equipment. Instead of heading for the beach or the snow with my friends on weekends I'd be at home listening to music and practising.

The great concert pianist, Paderewski, had just given a magnificent performance at Carnegie Hall in New York, when he was approached by a fan. "I'd give my life to play like that!" the man enthused, to which Paderewski replied soberly, "I did!" The majority of people will never know the price you paid for competence.

7. PURPOSE

Those who truly shine possess a purpose that ignites their passion. They have a preferred picture of the future and this vision drives them to see it fulfilled. There's nothing like goal posts to focus your sights and your energy. These people know what they want and are highly motivated to get it.

Genius is the infinite capacity for taking pains.

ALBERT EINSTEIN

If a man would move the world, he must first move himself.

SOCRATES

A PERFORMANCE THAT SHINES
a look into your future

Here are some questions to ponder. Take a pen and a journal and spend some time dreaming about your future. Write down your thoughts.

Five years from now…
What would you like to be able to do?
What kind of person would you like to be?
What do you want to be able to do with your gift? (Create for fun, create to move people and inspire them, create to help people worship, be able to communicate through your gift…)
What do you want to be able to impart?
What responses do you want to evoke in people?
Do you want to be an outstanding example?
Are you willing to pay the price?
Are you patient and persistent enough to last through the process?
What steps are you taking right now to take you on the journey that will lead you to that destination?

MASTERY

Those who have won the right to influence, inspire and delight, are those who, with an unceasing commitment to excellence, have taken their skills from raw talent to complete competence. These people are often referred to as masters.

Mastery can be defined as possessing consummate skill or having full command of a subject. It means having victory or complete control over. It is where an action is so natural that it does not require conscious thought to execute. A phrase that is often voiced when in the presence of a master is, "They make it look so easy!"

Mastery always begins with the basics. In most arts and professions these basics comprise the majority of the work. The special finishing touches and the elements that give a work character will never be masterful if the foundations they are built on are not.

This is what former CEO of Proctor and Gamble, Ed Artz, has to say on the subject: *"Mastering the fundamentals of any profession, be it in the arts, sports, or business, requires great sacrifice, endless repetition, and a*

Life is something like a trumpet. If you don't put anything in, you won't get anything out.

W. C. HANDY

If people knew how hard I worked to get my mastery, it wouldn't seem so wonderful after all.

MICHELANGELO

constant search for the best way to do things…. A professional in search of mastery brings an attitude to his or her work that no sacrifice is too great, and no experience or grunt work too menial if it helps achieve mastery of the fundamentals…. It all begins with attitude, striving to attain professionalism and embracing a winning way of life."[13]

As we have seen, mastery is neither automatic nor immediate. You have to start with what you have and apply focussed, consistent and quality effort. Practice and perseverance will eventually pay off.

The real master in the art of living makes little distinction between his art and his leisure. He simply pursues his vision of excellence in whatever he does, leaving others to decide whether he is working or playing. To him he is always doing both.

UNKNOWN

If one is master of one thing and undertands one thing well, one has at the same time, insight into and understanding of many things.

VINCENT VAN GOGH

prayer

Excellent and all-powerful God, thank You for putting in me a hunger for what is good. I want to gain mastery of myself and of my skills. Please help me to develop the gifts and talents You gave me, to the point where they are inspirational to others and honouring to Your name. I want to be an outstanding example for Your glory. Amen.

contract
Commitment to Competence

I, _____, commit to the pursuit of excellence and to the increase of my competence. I will work hard to master the skills I use to create so I can communicate with clarity and conviction.

Signature _____ Date _____

ENDNOTES

1. 1 Chronicles 15:22 Kenaniah, the head Levite, was chosen as the choir leader because of his skill.
   1 Chronicles 25:6-7 All these men were under the direction of their fathers as they made music at the house of the LORD. Their responsibilities included the playing of cymbals, lyres, and harps at the house of God. Asaph, Jeduthun, and Heman reported directly to the king. They and their families were all trained in making music before the LORD, and each of them - 288 in all - was an accomplished musician.
   1 Chronicles 15:22 Kenaniah, the head Levite, was chosen as the choir leader because of his skill.
   2 Chronicles 2:7 "So send me a master craftsman who can work with gold, silver, bronze, and iron; someone who is expert at dyeing purple, scarlet, and blue cloth; and a skilled engraver who can work with the craftsmen of Judah and Jerusalem who were selected by my father, David."
   2 Chronicles 30:22 Hezekiah encouraged the Levites for the skill they displayed as they served the LORD.
   See also; Psalms 33:3 Sing new songs of praise to him; play skilfully on the harp and sing with joy.
2. Daniel 6:3
3. Daniel 6:4
4. Colossians 3:23
5. Peterson, Eugene H: *The Message*, Navpress, Colorado Springs, CO,1993, p328
   Romans 12:1-2
6. As quoted in: *Sparks of Genius*; Robert and Michèle Root-Bernstein, Mariner Books, Boston, 2001, p22
7. Guitarist Steve Vai, as quoted in *Masters of Music*: Conversations with Berklee Greats, by Mark Small and Andrew Taylor © 2001 Berklee Press
   Steve Vai (Berklee '79) has toured and recorded with Frank Zappa, David Lee Roth, and Whitesnake, and has released a number of successful albums as a solo artist. He has acted in and composed music for the films Crossroads and Bill and Ted's Excellent Adventure, among others.
8. Baker, Philip: *Attitudes Of Amazing Achievers*, Webb & Partners, Perth, Australia, 2000, p62.
9. Phillipians 4:8
10. Proverbs 22:29 NASB
11. Buzan, Tony: *The Power Of Creative Intelligence*, Thorsons, London, 2001, p83.
12. This is based on Jeremiah 29:11
13. Charles Decker, *P&G 99: 99 Principles and Practices of Proctor and Gamble's Success*, HarperCollinsBusiness, London, 1998, p73.

continual growth

an increasing ability to shine

continual growth

VALUING GROWTH

Those who shine are able to do so because they have made growth a value in their lives. They've taken their gifts and natural abilities and purposefully extended and expanded them. They have pursued an increased capacity of both mind and body, enlarging their thinking and sharpening their skills.

A continuing and increasing ability to shine requires a commitment to perpetual growth. Remaining vital and effective means accepting the challenge to be a life-long learner.

There are countless millions of people with the potential to be extraordinary, inspirational and influential. Unfortunately, only a small portion of these ever become the shining lights they could be. They simply don't want to pay the price. The 18th Century German philosopher and writer, Johann von Goethe said, *"Everybody wants to be somebody; nobody wants to grow."*

Leadership guru, John Maxwell says, *"People are funny; they want to get ahead and succeed, but they are reluctant to change. They are often willing to grow only enough to accommodate their problems; instead, they need to grow enough to achieve their potential."*[1]

In a healthy organism, growth is natural. Living things grow; that's the way God designed them. For a normal, healthy person it's pretty difficult not to learn and grow in understanding and experience as the days go by. It should happen automatically.

Some people, however, grow a vast amount more than others because they are attentive, diligent and intentional about learning.

PRODUCING GROWTH

Growth is always a result of investment. To invest in something is to intentionally put money, effort, time, energy or thought into it to make a profit, gain an advantage, increase its value or achieve growth. If we invest in our gifts they will develop and increase.

People who place a high degree of value on growth become skilled investors. Here are seven characteristics of effective investors;

1. Good investors take investment seriously. It is a high priority for them, and the prospect of growth, increase and improvement motivates them.

2. Good investors are intentional about growth realising that they can influence their outcomes. They understand that *"The future is not a result of choices among alternative paths offered by the present, but a place that is created - created first in mind and will, created next in activity. The future is not some place we are going to, but one we are creating. The paths to it are not found but made, and the activity of making them changes both the maker and the destination."*[2]

3. Good investors understand that they have to do something to see growth. They know they'll have to work hard, think hard, make decisions, take risks and make sacrifices. They don't sit back and hope it will happen all by itself.

4. Good investors realise that risk is inevitable. They know you can never achieve great increase without the possibility of loss, and that not to invest is the greatest risk of all.

5. Good investors get great returns. They learn to spot great opportunities and to discern the best places to invest.

6. Good investors maximise their growth. They nourish their investment, providing it with the most favourable environment and conditions to give it the best possible chance of increase.

7. Good investors know the status of their investment at all times. As Proverbs 27:23 says, *"Know the state of your flocks, and put your heart into caring for your herds."*

CHOOSING TO INVEST

To really grow you have to want to! You have to want to be above average, desire to be extraordinary. You have to be dissatisfied with mediocre, with what's normal. You have to expect more from yourself and be prepared to do what it takes to deliver more. You must be unwilling to stay where you are. American President, Abraham Lincoln said, *"I do not think much of a man who is not wiser today than he was yesterday."*

If we choose to grow, and accept the challenge to become all we can be, it will mean the end of a comfortable existence, but also the beginning of a life of far greater reward.

Getting outside your comfort zone will introduce change and challenge to your life. We've all heard of "growing pains" - probably all had them when we hit adolescence. Attempting something beyond what you've already mastered will mean stretching and pain, but the bodybuilder's mantra, "no pain, no gain" is true. We simply can't have growth without some form of discomfort.

There will be exposure to opposition and criticism. Where there is motion there is always friction. As businessman J. Willard Marriott said, *"Good timber does not grow with ease. The stronger the wind, the stronger the trees."* Not everyone will agree with you, and some may even criticise. Take a look at the opinion polls for preferred Prime Minister or President and take heart. If you have a majority you are doing really well! We must accept that we can never please all of the people all of the time.

Of course, trying something new can be risky, so choosing to grow will certainly mean exposure to risk. Proverbs paints a great picture though when it says, *"An empty stable stays clean, but no income comes from an empty stable."*[3] And in another place it talks about the lazy person who stays in saying, *"If I go outside, I might meet a lion in the street and be killed!"*[4] To make anything of our lives we must be willing to take risks. The greater the potential for breakthrough or success, the greater the risk factor.

Choosing to grow will mean choosing to make sacrifices. John Maxwell has a saying - *"You've got to give up to go up"*. To go to a new level we will have to leave something behind. If we want to do a part time course one night a week, we will have to give up several hours of television, or going out with friends, or whatever we may normally do on that night. It will cost us something, but what we pay for we get to keep.

INVESTMENT RETURNS

We should take investing in our personal lives and abilities seriously. Here are some of the reasons why we need to put time, effort and money into our gifts:

> *To increase our capacity to influence others positively;*
> *To become more competent - we'll then perform better;*
> *To become more confident (and therefore perform better);*
> *To fulfil tasks with more ease and less stress;*
> *To become a bigger person and have more to give;*
> *Because you can't lead if you're not out in front;*
> *Growth brings with it great reward:*
>> *sense of achievement and fulfilment;*
>> *honour; "Do you see a man skilled in his work? He will stand before kings." Proverbs 22:29;*
> *To experience a better, larger, more fulfilling future;*
> *To reach our potential;*
> *Because we're accountable to God for what we've been given.*

Am I taking my personal growth seriously?
Am I being intentional about investing into who I am becoming?
Do I have a plan?
What is it?

RESPONSIBILITY TO GROW

Our God-given talents and abilities are not without obligation. It is our duty to exercise and expand them. *"The capacity for art, beauty, creativity, and artistic experience is something people should cultivate."*[5]

Jesus illustrates this point clearly in the Parable of the Talents.[6] He tells about a Master who goes on a long trip. Before he leaves, he calls in three servants and gives each of them talents (money). He gives them different amounts of talents but the same instructions; "Invest this for me." Two of the servants go out and do the best they can, investing the talents to see an increase. When the Master returns, they bring back twice as much as he had sent them out with. The third, because of laziness, fear, disobedience or whatever reason, did nothing with his talent but keep it hidden, and as a result could only present the Master with the potential he was given in the first place. The Master was angry and ended up taking even that from him.

There are no victories at bargain prices.

Dwight D. Eisenhower

When we are really honest with ourselves we must admit our lives are all that really belong to us. So it is how we use our lives that determines the kind of men we are.

Cesar Chavez

The message is clear: We are responsible for what we have been given. You are responsible to develop your potential. I must develop mine. We must accept personal responsibility for this.

FOCUS AREAS FOR INVESTMENT

John Maxwell suggests four areas we can grow in:

1. Attitudes
Everything starts with our thinking. Our attitudes determine how we act.

2. Relationships
The ability to relate and interact with others is important in everything we do.

3. Leadership
Our effectiveness depends on how well we can lead others.

4. Personal and professional skills
Skills on their own are not much, but built on a platform of good attitude, people skills and ability to lead, produce an extraordinary person.

Every part of our life will benefit from development, but there is an order of priority. We need to grow from the inside out. Great attitude is superior to great ability. Character is more important than skill. Spiritual health is a higher priority than physical health. The core of us - our engine room - what makes us the way we are, must be maintained and nurtured first before we can show the results outwardly.

INVESTMENT TIPS
an exercise in how to grow

Look over the following suggestions and mark the ones you could put into action or increase your commitment to.
1. *Be teachable, have an open heart to constructive criticism and honest feedback.*
2. *Ask your team leader for input (and be prepared to receive it).*
3. *Be accountable to someone for your growth in a certain area.*
4. *Be eager to learn:*
    i. *Get lessons (you go further faster with a teacher).*
    ii. *Read books.*

      iii.   Read relevant magazines.
      iv.   Check the internet for resources.

5. *Practise.*
6. *Study.*
7. *Share.*
8. *Collaborate.*
9. *Keep your eyes open, look for opportunities that will stretch you.*
10. *Set some goals.*
11. *Be prepared to change.*
12. *Be prepared to sacrifice (give up to go up).*
13. *Be prepared to sow.*
14. *Read John Maxwell's book, "Be All You Can Be".[7]*
15. *Be attentive, diligent and intentional about growth.*
16. *Get around people who will help you grow, help challenge your thinking, your skill level.*
17. *Focus on small pieces and get them right before moving on.*

Now look back over the list again and decide which three points you will start with. Number them in order of priority. Now ask, "What can I do today to begin making this happen?"

_____

_____

_____

_____

_____

A SUCCESSFUL JOURNEY

We need to understand that success is not a place of arrival but a journey of quality decisions and experiences. Success doesn't just "fall" on you. It won't sneak up behind you and surprise you. It follows persistent discipline and consistently doing the right thing even when it's not the easiest thing. *"Success is not the result of a miracle! True success is the result of making the right choices, performing the right actions, and instilling the right disciplines."[8]* Success is the process of changing for the better. Godly success sees the big picture and takes a long view.

We also have to accept that growth and positive progress will have their costs and associated pains. *"Not too many people are willing to pay the price on a consistent basis, with reliability, and keeping with the plan.*

There are no shortcuts to success. It takes hard work. The only place where success appears before work is in the dictionary."[9]

DREAM INVESTMENT

What, in your life, are you investing in?

_____

_____

_____

Are you being responsible with what you've been given?

_____

_____

_____

Which of your dreams will go unfulfilled unless you get serious about growing?

_____

_____

_____

QUALITIES OF A SUCCESSFUL INVESTOR:

1. Discipline

The word alone is enough to strike fear into most hearts. It has negative connotations for most of us because it brings to mind hard work, difficult circumstances, uncomfortable situations, pain, blood, sweat and tears! And yet the greatest of those to live on this earth have been people of great discipline. They are the ones who have learned to overcome the enchanted call of sleep and the gravity-like pull towards comfort.

Lack of discipline will override talent. Talent is an indicator of potential that, without discipline, will come to nothing. There are millions of highly talented people around the world whose true potential will never be known because they have not been able to master themselves.

Discipline is simply the ability to bring emotions, skills, attitudes and strength under the direction of our will. It is enduring discomfort with the knowledge that we are becoming a bigger, better, more capable person. It is, as John Maxwell puts it, *"doing what you really don't want to do so that you can do what you really want to do."*[10] *"Discipline means doing the right things at the right time for the right reason."*[11]

Discipline is result-driven. It's all about the application of the will to achieve a desired result. When there is something I am convinced I want to achieve, desire produces the motivation to be disciplined. Discipline, then, is a by-product of compelling vision or conviction.

One of the things that motivates me to be disciplined, is understanding the concept summed up in this statement by Jim Rohn: *"For every disciplined effort, there are multiple rewards."*

This is a biblical principle. The Bible says, *"What you sow you will reap."*[12] You always reap more than you sow, because seed grows - it multiplies. Sowing small efforts of discipline with consistency will build a powerful life that reaps benefits in every area - effectiveness, influence, productivity and fulfilment.

Nothing happens in isolation. For every action there is a consequence. Every encounter we have with others affects them for eternity. It is inspiring to realise that every disciplined effort we make will positively impact on our life and the lives of others.

Motivate yourself to be disciplined by prophesying your future and the results of your efforts. Have a vision of what could be and let it inspire you into action.

The Bible says, *"Let us not become weary in doing good, for at the proper time we will reap a harvest if we do not give up."*[13] In other words, don't become weary of making consistent disciplined efforts, for they will result in great and multiple rewards.

SELF-MASTERY

Some disciplines to develop:

> *Have a quiet time every day - go to The Source of all good and nourish your soul.*
> *Learn.*
> *To learn, you must love discipline; it is stupid to hate correction. Proverbs 12:1*
> *Read good books. Choose them wisely.*
> *Charlie "Tremendous" Jones says, "You will be the same person in 5 years time except for the books you read and the people you meet".*
> *Study something - grow your knowledge.*
> *Intelligent people are always open to new ideas. In fact, they look for them. Proverbs 18:15*
> *Get out of bed - don't use the snooze button.*
> *Exercise - we've got to be in good shape to love well.*
> *Have a healthy diet - we are what we eat.*
> *Watch your mental diet (entertainment) - we are what we think.*
> *A wise person is hungry for truth, while the fool feeds on trash. Proverbs 15:14*
> *Grow your skill - practise your instrument, your craft…*
> *Finish what you start. Work at something rather than giving up easily - be persistent. Try and try again.*
> *Plan ahead and set schedules.*
> *Be on time (for everything):*
>> *For appointments*
>> *Paying bills*
>> *For work*
>> *For rehearsals*
> *Do the best you can - always. This eliminates regret.*
> *Keep your promises.*
> *Think before you speak.*
> *He who guards his mouth and his tongue keeps himself from calamity. Proverbs 21:23 (NIV), or as the NLT puts it, If you keep your mouth shut, you will stay out of trouble. The godly think before speaking; the wicked spout evil words. Proverbs 15:28*
> *Speak life.*
> *Those who love to talk will experience the consequences, for the tongue can kill or nourish life. Proverbs 18:21*
> *A person's words can be life-giving water; words of true wisdom are as refreshing as a bubbling brook. Proverbs 18:4*
> *Think positive.*
> *Fix your thoughts on what is true and honourable and right. Think about things that are pure and lovely and admirable. Think about things that are excellent and worthy of praise. Philippians 4:8*
> *Pay attention - don't go through life so engrossed in your own issues that you miss opportunities to be a blessing.*

I count him braver who overcomes his desires than him who conquers his enemies; for the hardest victory is over self.

ARISTOTLE

You need the room, you need the door, and you need the determination to shut the door. You need a concrete goal, as well. The longer you keep to these basics, the easier the act of writing will become. Don't wait for the muse.

STEPHEN KING

Two areas I can begin improving immediately are:

1. _____

2. _____

_____

LEVELS OF DISCIPLINE

There are three possible levels of discipline:

First: Imposed by outside authority (involuntary)
Second: Self-imposed (voluntary)
Third: Invited from outside authority (voluntary)

Everyone has to submit to the first level - we don't really have any choice in these matters. For example, to drive a car safely on the city streets, requires us to observe road rules whether we agree with them or not. Or, as school children we must fulfil the expectations of our teachers (often against our wills!)

The next level comes with maturity. We begin to understand that the pain of discipline is easier to bear than the pain of regret. It is better to experience by my own intention a little discomfort now, than to suffer indiscriminately later at the hands of circumstance. As Jim Rohn says, *"The most valuable form of discipline is the one that you impose upon yourself. Don't wait for things to deteriorate so drastically that someone else must impose discipline in your life."*

Good people submit themselves to the discipline of others, but great people have learned to discipline themselves.

Of course, each level includes the one before. The third level is added to levels one and two. This level is occupied by outstanding individuals whose light shines ever brighter as the years go by. They understand self-discipline well. They're also honest enough to know that they have blind spots and weaknesses, and to reach their full potential they'll need the help of others. They find mentors and teachers whom they can trust to lead them in the right direction, and submit themselves to their authority.

Great people have learned to discipline themselves, but outstanding people also invite the input of others and make themselves accountable to them.

MOVING ON UP
an exercise in letting go

As leadership specialist John Maxwell says, "You've got to give up to go up."
Go through your wardrobe and throw out, pass on or donate anything you don't like or haven't worn for a year.
Make room for progress.
Go through your files and throw out anything that is now irrelevant.
Are there any pastimes that are hindering you from moving forward in your life? Make a commitment to change them.

---

2. Patience: Understanding Time and Process

Good investors know that returns take time to mature and that the process can be unpredictable. Growth is not always linear; progress is not always in a straight line. Sometimes we might feel we're progressing in leaps and bounds, while other times it seems like we're slipping backwards.

In preparation for a live recording I was going through some ideas for a guitar solo that I would have to perform. I was quite surprised at some of the ideas I was coming up with and how well I was playing. It surprised me because I had not recently been doing any serious practice or learning anything new about soloing. I have noticed this several times over the years. What seems to happen is that things you learn and practise continue to seep in for many months, maybe even years.

If I accept this as true, it helps motivate me to be continually learning something new and to not be too impatient about seeing the results of my practice. It may seem like I'm not making great progress, but it is happening and the full effect of what I'm learning now won't be experienced until long after I've forgotten I was even learning it. It's like osmosis.

It's like a small bucket with a couple of tiny holes, inside a larger bucket. Water (information), is poured into the smaller bucket (representing the learning area of the brain) and begins to seep out of the holes into the larger bucket, becoming part of my experience. How much I can hold in the smaller bucket depends on how attentive I am to the information. How much I can hold in the larger bucket is virtually unlimited. (The holes in the smaller bucket can be enlarged by continuing to practise and study the information.)

The point is that we don't experience the full extent of the benefits of our study and practice until we have been through the process. Time is involved.

TAKING CONTROL

Three areas of my life I want to be more disciplined about are:

1. _____

2. _____

3. _____

The first step I am going to take towards mastering each area is:

1. _____

2. _____

3. _____

3. Diligence

If discipline says, "just do it", diligence says, "do it well". Diligence is the ability to focus our energies and give attention to getting things right. It's persisting with difficult exercises, being thorough and not cutting corners. When we are diligent we are committed to finishing what we start and to doing it to the very best of our ability. Diligence understands the importance of sticking with the programme until the process is complete.

Diligence is also to do with intentional consistency. It will cause us to practise - to take action repetitively for the purpose of improvement. It will cause us to form healthy and helpful habits.

HABITS

Habit is one of the most powerful forces in our lives. If we learn to harness this power we can begin to form the kind of future we want. Champions are those who have the habits of champions. The writer of the following piece certainly understood this.

I am your constant companion.
I am your greatest helper or heaviest burden.
I will push you onward or drag you down to failure.
I am completely at your command.

Half the things you do you might as well turn over to me and I will be able to do them quickly and correctly.

I am easily managed - you must merely be firm with me.
Show me exactly how you want something done and after a few lessons I will do it automatically.
I am the servant of all great men; and alas, of all failures as well.
Those who are great, I have made great.
Those who are failures, I have made failures.

I am not a machine, though I work with all the precision of a machine plus the intelligence of a man.
You may run me for a profit or run me for ruin - it makes no difference to me.

Take me, train me, be firm with me, and I will place the world at your feet.
Be easy with me and I will destroy you.
Who am I? I am Habit!
ANONYMOUS

HABIT REPLACEMENT
exchanging the bad for the better

List 3 bad habits, (Ok, 5!) List the obvious and the subtle. (If you can't think of 5 ask your friends!)

1. _____
2. _____
3. _____
4. _____
5. _____

A piece of art is the surface expression of a life lived within productive patterns.

DAVID BAYLES AND TED ORLAND

Remember that you become what you practise most…. It makes sense, then, to be careful what you practise.

RICHARD CARLSON

Which one do you hate the most?

Start with that and take a step towards replacing it with a good habit. What habit will you replace it with?

How will you begin?

Achievement is bought on the time-payment plan, with a new instalment required each day.

J. Oswald Sanders

GEARING UP FOR GROWTH

This is important: You must believe that growth is possible for you, and that it will happen. Remember, growth is a process not an event. The only way to grow is in small increments. Trying to grow in giant leaps will just frustrate us and give us a hernia! I read somewhere recently that it is easier to walk 10 feet than to jump 10 feet. Try it! Now try doing it several times in a row. What a great illustration! One step at a time, at a reasonable pace, will help us finish the journey.

Wise men and women are always learning, always listening for fresh insights.

Proverbs 18:15
The Message

There's a certain intoxication that comes when we learn a little and see the results of that learning. Our confidence begins to rise and our performance improves. Soon we are thirsting for more, and before we know it we are addicted to learning and growing. Starting is the hardest part but generally, once we begin, motivation will not be an issue.

The happiest people in the world are growing people - those who stretch to go faster, higher, longer, to be stronger, better, more accurate. We foster a sense of fulfilment and achievement when we are growing.

Actually, the happiest are those who go a step further. They turn their efforts outward to improve not only themselves, but others too. They thrive on seeing others grow and develop towards their potential.

If we want to shine, we must have a growth mentality, a desire to progress and become all we can. Growing people are the ones who inspire us and truly have the ability to impact the lives of others.

SMALL STEPS

Make a checklist of ten small things you would like to change in your life (e.g., buy a new pen, organise my CD collection…)

1. _____
2. _____
3. _____
4. _____
5. _____
6. _____
7. _____
8. _____
9. _____
10. _____

Choose two and make them a reality today!

The roots of education are bitter, but the fruit is sweet.

ARISTOTLE

Did you ever observe to whom the accidents happen? Chance favours only the prepared mind.

LOUIS PASTEUR

prayer

Infinite Wonderful God, I want to always be increasing in my ability to shine for You. I want to become all I can and fulfil all You have made me for. Help me to continue to develop disciplines and habits in my life that will keep me learning and growing. Amen.

Commitment To Continual Growth

I, _____, am determined to expand my life, to develop my spiritual and natural gifts making them increasingly "give-able". I will discipline myself and develop habits that will continually stretch me and keep me moving forward in life. I will enlist the help of a teacher, mentor or coach to maximise my potential growth.

Signature _____   Date _____

ENDNOTES

1. Maxwell, John: *Becoming a Person of Influence*, Thomas Nelson Publishers, Nashville; 1997, p126.
2. John Schaar
3. Proverbs 14:4
4. Proverbs 22:13
5. Leland Ryken, *The Liberated Imagination*: Thinking Christianly About The Arts, 1989, Harold Shaw Publishers, Wheaton, Illinois, p16.
6. Parable of the Talents (Matthew 25:14-30)
7. Maxwell, John: *Be All You Can Be*; Victor Books, Wheaton, IL; 1987.
8. Strand, Robert: *Success Without Guilt*; New Leaf Press, Green Forest, AR; 1997, p53.
9. ibid, p61.
10. John Maxwell, *The 17 Essential Qualities of a Team Player*; Thomas Nelson Publishers, Nashville; 2002, p57.
11. ibid, p61.
12. Galatians 6:7 Do not be deceived: God cannot be mocked. A man reaps what he sows. NLT
13. Galatians 6:9 NLT

character
shining from the inside out

character

When we speak of character in someone we are generally speaking of the total collection of qualities that make up their individuality. In this chapter we will approach the subject of character by looking at the essential features and distinctive marks of a person who shines from the inside out.

Great character is a fascinating fabric woven from numerous personal qualities. It should be colourful and strong, shot through with intriguing individuality and nuance. A sound and vivid character is the very core of a shining life. Its formation should be one of our most passionate pursuits.

Confidence is wonderful and competence is important, but they're only a part of the pie. If what we produce is to have real substance, sound character is essential, since what is created is always imprinted with the image of its creator.

Throughout the ages creative people have come under fire for having questionable character. Rory Noland, in his excellent book, The Heart Of The Artist noted: *"Unfortunately there are certain negative stereotypes that are attached to people with artistic temperaments. Some people say that we are temperamental and eccentric. Some people think we're difficult and strange. Some might say we are moody and emotionally unstable. Others see us as free-spirited, quirky, and undisciplined. Excuses are often made for the shortcomings of the artistic temperament. The problem occurs when we artists buy into those excuses and use them to justify unacceptable behaviour."*[1]

Artistic people can tend to be more sensitive, passionate, introverted and in touch with their feelings than the average person. These qualities are good and can help us in our art, but there is a danger if they are not kept in balance. Character must be built on firmer foundations than what and how we feel.

Some may argue that great character is not essential to creation and art making. However, it is of profound import to the formation of friendship and the establishment of reputation. For meaningful interaction with others and effective influence, character is vital. We need to shine clearly, not only in what we do but also in who we are.

ON DISPLAY

Character is observable. It is seen and judged by those around us. Great character inspires confidence in others. It will make people want to partner with you. They know they'll find you a pleasure to work with. They'll know they can trust you. They'll know you can be counted on to add value to any endeavour you partner in.

Crisis reveals character because character is revealed through actions. How we respond to challenges, trials, successes and failures will expose our real nature. Strong character will sustain you through failure and keep you balanced in success.

In this chapter we'll examine some of the qualities that can combine in the crucible of time and testing to form noble character.

REPUTATION AND LEGACY

Five things I would like to be known for (while I'm alive):

1. _____
2. _____
3. _____
4. _____
5. _____

Five things I would like to be remembered for (after I'm gone):

1. _____
2. _____

Our character is what we do when we think no one is looking.

H. JACKSON BROWN, JR.

Reputation is what men and women think of us; character is what God and angels know of us.

THOMAS PAINE

3. _____

4. _____

5. _____

INTEGRITY

Integrity is the cornerstone of great character. It is without doubt the single most important quality with which to build character.

Integrity cannot be bought; a nice suit doesn't prove you have it. Integrity is not image or reputation for these can be falsely presented. Neither is it based on accomplishment for many can get things done.

Integrity is proven over time through consistency. It is built by the small choices we make every moment, to do what is right every time. It is demonstrated when people can see that what we think, what we say and what we do are all in line with each other. The great Greek philosopher Socrates said, *"The first key to greatness is to be in reality what we appear to be."*

Thomas Macauley linked character and integrity when he said, *"The measure of a man's real character is what he would do if he would never be found out."* Wow! It is certainly easier to take the way of least resistance when you think no one will know, but compromise is the assassin of character. Temptations come to all of us but integrity proves itself by remaining intact through the toughest of tests.

Dependability

Dependability is closely tied to integrity. You can count on people who are dependable. You can believe what they say; you don't have to take it with a grain of salt, or read between the lines. They're honest, trustworthy and consistent. They are not just interested - they're committed. They won't "pass the buck". They'll be on time and they'll know their stuff. They are the kind of person everyone wants on their team. In short, they're awesome and there are not enough of them! Make the decision to be a dependable person.

Integrity's Payoff

If you have integrity with people they will trust you. They will listen to you and be influenced by what you say. They will be inspired by you and will follow your leadership. So integrity is important to your relationships and your ability to influence.

It is also valuable for your peace of mind. This is how Zig Ziglar explains it: *"Now the beautiful thing about integrity, when integrity is part of you as a person and is part of your life, you do the right thing. When you do the right thing, you have nothing to feel guilty about. With integrity you have nothing to fear because you have nothing to hide. Now think about it, with guilt and fear both removed from your back, doesn't it just make sense that you can function more effectively?"* Live with integrity and have no regrets.

Proving Integrity

Integrity is about consistency. It's about "always" and "never". To be a person of integrity you need to demonstrate over a period of time that what you say is what you mean and isn't made respectable by judicious omissions, or spiced up with tasty exaggerations. You'll have to show that your talk and your walk line up.

You'll need to establish that you're not selfish. Selfishness will weave a crookedness into everything you say or do. Selfishness will tend to "tip the balance" in your favour and colour your decisions, quickly leading to compromise.

People need to know they can depend on you to respond to similar situations in similar fashion. They want to see that you're the same person no matter where you are or who you're with.

Integrity demands that you do the "right" thing every time, rather than the easiest thing or the thing that's best for you, whether it's a large or small issue.

BUILDING INTEGRITY

Here are some tips on how to build integrity in your life:
> *Keep your priorities in line - don't be led by your feelings.*
> *Check your motives for doing things.*
> *Work hard at not being selfish.*
> *Do what you say you'll do. Be dependable.*
> *Don't lie. Tell the truth even if it hurts - can people believe everything you say? Be undeviatingly honest.*
> *Be honest about your own weaknesses.*

> Don't be a pretender - be honest about what you don't know or can't do.
> Keep accountable to others and hold yourself accountable. Don't be secretive.
> Be transparent.
> Be self disciplined to do the right thing - don't wait for others to catch you out or tell you to get it together.
> Ask yourself the questions you hope no one ever asks you (and answer them honestly).
> Never betray trust. Value confidentiality.
> Remember that "you are the message" - people will hear what you say but they'll believe what you do.

Remember, integrity cannot be faked. You may fool some people some of the time but you'll eventually be left red-faced. Robert Strand concurs; *"To fail at integrity is to fail at everything else. You can be talented, knowledgeable, capable, gifted, successful, and have remarkable abilities. However, if you are not believed to be a person of integrity, you will not be trusted. You will eventually fail. Cleverness and brilliance can take you a long way in public life, for a time, but in the long run it all fails miserably unless the brilliance is matched by the character trait of integrity."*[2]

GOLDEN RULE OF INTEGRITY: DO THE RIGHT THING - EVERY TIME!

INTEGRITY CHECK

1. How well do I treat people from whom I can gain nothing?
2. Am I transparent with others?
3. Do I role-play based on the person(s) I'm with?
4. Am I the same person when I'm in the spotlight as I am when I'm alone?
5. Do I quickly admit wrongdoing without being pressed to do so?
6. Do I put other people ahead of my personal agenda?
7. Do I have an unchanging standard for moral decisions, or do circumstances determine my choices?
8. Do I make difficult decisions, even when they have a personal cost attached to them?
9. When I have something to say about people, do I talk to them or about them?
10. Am I accountable to at least one other person for what I think, say, and do?

Don't be too quick to respond to the questions. If character development is a serious area of need in your life, your tendency may be to skim through the questions, giving answers

If we keep ourselves long enough under the right influences, slowly and surely we shall find that we can form habits that will develop us along the line of those influences.

OSWALD CHAMBERS

Let the world know you as you are, not as you think you should be, because sooner or later, if you are posing, you will forget the pose, and then where are you?

FANNY BRICE

that describe how you wish you were rather than who you actually are. Take some time to reflect on each question, honestly considering it before answering. Then work on the areas where you're having the most trouble.
(Taken from Becoming a Person of Influence, John Maxwell & Jim Dornan. Pg 24)[3]

HUMILITY
Teachability

Humility is the heart of teachability. It is an attitude that is open and lacking arrogance. Teachable people are totally aware that they don't know everything. They're eager to learn, curious, always asking questions, approaching life with a beginner's mindset.

Truly teachable people are able to admit to their mistakes; they don't automatically begin offering excuses or passing blame. When presented with suggestions and constructive criticism they are not defensive but welcome the input, ready to grow. Defensive reactions can very quickly bring the ugliest out of us. It is much better to stay calm and keep our mouths shut.

No one likes a know-it-all. When we display a teachable spirit others will warm to us knowing that we will respect their opinions and value their input. We become more of a pleasure to work with.

The day we stop being teachable is the day when we stop learning and growing - and the day our lamp begins to burn out.

ADMIRATION

Who are 5 people you admire greatly?

1. _____
2. _____
3. _____
4. _____
5. _____

What could you learn from them?

_____

_____

_____

Visit a bookstore or Library and find a Biography of one of these people. Read it!

_____

DEALING WELL WITH CRITICISM

If you want to shine in life and stand out from the crowd, you can count on your share of criticism. Aristotle put it well, *"Criticism is something you can avoid easily by saying nothing, doing nothing, and being nothing."*

Criticism is a fact of life. It can confront us at any time and rarely waits for an invitation. Part of the composition of a robust character is the ability to deal well with criticism of any kind.

As a creative person, learning to respond well to criticism is vital because creativity can only thrive in a nurturing, supportive environment. Creative ideas, when they are young, are easily scorched by a few untempered words. And the ideas themselves are not all that get burned. It doesn't take many of these harsh encounters for us to withdraw like a sea anemone, refusing to venture out into the vulnerable territory of public creativity. Before long our gift has been buried and our light snuffed out.

Criticism will come, but it is always up to us what we do with it - and perhaps, what we allow it to do to us. We can choose to accept or reject it, act on it or ignore it. We have to learn how to take the "heat" out of it so it doesn't damage us but make us stronger.

We must learn to discern the difference between constructive and destructive criticism. You can normally tell by the spirit in which it is given. Constructive criticism will be given out of a desire to help you grow and improve. It will be given privately and in a gentle and nurturing manner.

Destructive criticism is the kind intended to tear down, embarrass and belittle. It will generally appear as derision and is most often delivered by someone who is hurting, or jealous, or someone who has developed a consistently negative and cynical approach to life.

A successful man is one who can lay a firm foundation with the bricks others have thrown at him.

DAVID BRINKLEY, TELEVISION JOURNALIST

Honest criticism is hard to take, particularly from a relative, a friend, an acquaintance or a stranger.

FRANKLIN JONES

If someone offers us constructive criticism, it is because they can see more for us than we are currently experiencing. Try hard not to take it personally. Remember, their comments are directed at your art, not your heart. Don't be defensive but see it as a chance to learn, an opportunity to improve. Always keep an open heart.

Be honest with yourself - is it valid? Many times we need others to tell us what we already know deep down to be true and in need of attention. We need to be humble and thank our friends for being courageous enough to speak into our life.

On the other hand, if you believe you've received criticism that is unfounded, stamp "reject" on it, toss it out and move on! But not before you've checked it out with someone you can trust to be honest with you. Don't get mad or try to get even; if you are right, time will prove it.

Who is the critic? Is he or she qualified to make an insightful and valid judgement? John Maxwell writes, *"Adverse criticism from a wise man is more to be desired than the enthusiastic approval of a fool."[4]*

Understand that everyone fails, and being criticised is not the end of the world. It is how we respond to it that matters. Even the greatest are criticised. Consider Jesus, who was pure-hearted and without sin, who experienced the ultimate destructive criticism - persecution and death. Galileo, like Copernicus before him, was ridiculed and called a heretic because he believed the world was round. Christopher Columbus faced the same mockery when he decided to prove this theory, believing he could reach India by sailing West from Europe, rather than East. When the Wright brothers, Wilbur and Orville, were working on their "aeroplane", people mocked them saying that if God had wanted human beings to fly, he would have given us feathers. Although Mozart is today considered the most universal of composers, having an incredible command of form, taste and range of expression, some of his music was called frivolous by some of the "serious" composers and critics of his day.

Not everyone wants to participate in your success. That's OK; just accept it. Build relationships with people who are positive and interested in your welfare. They will give you the right kind of criticism and help you deal with that which is undeserved.

TAKING THE HEAT
an exercise in dealing with criticism

What criticism have I received recently?

_____

_____

_____

Was it constructive?

_____

Was I defensive?

_____

Did I receive it well?

_____

How could I have handled it better?

_____

_____

_____

Whom have I learnt from in the last month?

_____

_____

What did I learn?

_____

_____

_____

_____

GRATITUDE

One great characteristic of humility is living life from a position of gratitude. This shows an acceptance of our "place" in the grand scheme of things. It's a recognition that I am not the source of my own power, I am not the provider of my own wealth or health; I am not the author of all the good in

I remind myself every morning: nothing I say this day will teach me anything. So if I'm going to learn, I must do it by listening.

LARRY KING

It is the dull man who is always sure, and the sure man who is always dull.

H. L. MENCKEN, WRITER

my life. I acknowledge that there is a greater power than I, that He is Good, and He's intentionally involved in my life.

The Bible tells us that God created all things and that everything belongs to Him.[5] Everything we have, including life itself, is a gift from God. When we understand this, how could we not wake up every day with a thankful heart?

Humility will also show in our ability to show gratitude to the people around us in recognition of all they bring into our lives. We do not live isolated and relationally disconnected lives. We must realise that our families and friends, and even people we have never met, are frequently responsible for enriching and empowering our lives. Gratitude will happily give credit where credit's due.

It's good for us to develop the attitude of gratitude, not only based on what we see we've been blessed with, but also on the fact of our own insufficiency. We must understand that we need outside help to live. This really is the basis of humility.

THE GOLDEN RULE OF HUMILITY: ALWAYS BE OPEN TO LEARNING FROM ANYONE AND ANYTHING.

ATTITUDE OF GRATITUDE

Am I a grateful person?

Could I cultivate thankfulness more in my life?

List 10 things/circumstances to be grateful for.

1. _____
2. _____
3. _____
4. _____
5. _____
6. _____
7. _____

8. _____

9. _____

10. _____

List 5 people to be grateful to:

1. _____

2. _____

3. _____

4. _____

5. _____

Send them a thank you note or card.

_____

INITIATIVE

Initiative is the power or ability to begin or to follow through energetically with a plan or task without prompting or direction from others. It is a quality found in all highly successful people. They don't wait for success to come looking for them, they actively pursue opportunities. They don't wait for someone else to have all the ideas and do all the work, but jump in with enthusiasm and do what they know has to be done.

Andrew Carnegie illustrated the importance of initiative in this statement; *"There are two types of people who never achieve much in their lifetime. The person who won't do what he is told, and the person who does no more than he is told."*

Recognising Initiative

People with initiative keep their sensory gates wide open; they "see" things. Best-selling Leadership writer, John Maxwell says, *"Leaders see further than everyone else and before everyone else."* I would add that leaders see because they are looking! Likewise, they hear because they are listening, they find out because they are asking, they're prepared because they are thinking, they know because they are learning. Their initiative keeps them ahead of the pack.

To display initiative you must have vision and see the big picture. You have to believe in the vision enough to act without being asked by someone else. You have to be motivated from within and be a self-starter. You can't be a procrastinator and an avoider of issues, trying to "turn a blind eye".

Initiative will have you asking questions when you don't know and learning from every experience whether success or failure. It will have you leading by example and acting early.

Initiators accept responsibility for the gifts and abilities they have. They don't believe in fate, understanding that they are in the driver's seat of their life. Success is their responsibility. This requires a certain amount of confidence and the belief that they are significant and what they do is significant. It realises that regular trips out of the comfort zone are important for growth and progress and the benefits are well worthwhile.

The Value Of Initiative

In a team situation initiative is a valuable commodity. It helps spread the load, easing the leader's burden - this is huge! More eyes see more things, and more hands make light work. Also, those who initiate set a great example and when others catch on, momentum is created.

Initiative will also add value to your own life, building confidence and a sense of achievement. When you initiate you attract opportunity. Doors begin to open and you seem to be in the right place at the right time more often. Your initiative will expose you to wider experience, enhancing your personal growth. It can be risky and scary but it is definitely worth it.

God Responds To Initiative

Jesus said, *"Everyone who asks, receives. Everyone who seeks, finds. And the door is opened to everyone who knocks."*[6] This is a clear statement of the value of initiative. People respond to initiative and so does God.

It's interesting to note that virtually all of the miracles Jesus did for people, were for those who called on Him or "came to Him".

GOLDEN RULE OF INITIATIVE: DO SOMETHING ABOUT IT, AND DO IT NOW.

INCREASING INITIATIVE

Here are some keys to living life as an initiator:

THINK POSITIVE
> *Initiative thrives where there is enthusiasm, energy and vigour*
> *Understand the results of initiative and the consequences of lack of initiative*

OPEN YOUR SENSORY GATES
> *See potential*
> *See opportunity*
> *See needs - what needs to be done?*
> *Listen to your inner voice*
> *Think ahead*

JUST DO IT!
> *Don't wait to be told!*
> *Overcome fears that keep you from acting*
> *The more you do it, the better you become*
> *Prepare for all possibilities*
> *Act - make it happen*

RESPONSIBILITY

This quality is very closely linked to initiative. In fact, those who show initiative prove that they are able to accept responsibility. Michael Korda recognized that *"Success on any major scale requires you to accept responsibility... in the final analysis, the one quality that all successful people have... is the ability to take on responsibility."* If we are to shine in life there will always be a cost. England's great war time leader, Sir Winston Churchill said, *"The price of greatness is responsibility."*

It is disturbing how many people espouse the philosophy: "if it feels good, do it!" Responsibility has nothing to do with how we feel. Accepting responsibility means we will do what needs to be done (and not do what shouldn't be done), whether we feel like it or not. We do it because it is right.

Likewise, responsibility is not related to convenience. Whether circumstances are favourable or not, we fulfil our obligations.

Being Responsible

If you are someone who accepts responsibility, you will set high standards for yourself and expect the same of others. You'll strive for excellence and encourage others to strive for excellence. You'll be on the look-out for ways to grow or improve yourself and the team.

Responsible people honour their commitments. They follow through to the end, staying with them under pressure, being persistent and not giving up without trying many possible ways of solving a problem. They are finishers.

People who are responsible have no problem with being accountable. They have nothing to hide because they are doing all that is expected of them and more. They don't have to live in fear of being caught out - they live with a clear conscience.

When we accept responsibility we won't say, "That's not my job." We must accept responsibility for whatever we have some degree of control over.

My Responsibilities

The Bible says, *"we are each responsible for our own conduct."*[7] We're lights in the world and we need to set an example in what we say and do. Our words and actions are constantly on display and it's important that we send the right messages.

The Bible is also clear about the need to accept responsibility for the stimulation, growth and use of our own gifts and talents, and for whatever work we have been given to do.[8]

We have to admit to our own mistakes and weaknesses, accepting that they are ours to do something about. We are not to be blame shifters, approaching life with a victim's mentality.

When we believe that we are meant to be a blessing to others, we'll take responsibility for the team's success. We'll want to speak positively and encourage each other, boosting the team's morale. We'll be interested in the wellbeing of others on the team, and committed to their personal success.

If we are to shine brightly we must work harder to see our responsibilities fulfilled than to see our rights fulfilled.

GOLDEN RULE OF RESPONSIBILITY: IF YOU SEE SOMETHING THAT NEEDS TO BE DONE, DO SOMETHING ABOUT IT.

A SPIRIT OF GENEROSITY

Of all the qualities for which one could have a reputation, generosity must surely hold the highest honour. To be generous encompasses so much that is positive and noble. Generosity is the very manifestation of love. It is love out loud!

Look at these similes for the word generous:
abundant, ample, above expectation, more than required, excessive, rich, big-hearted, open-handed, extravagant, unselfish, munificent, liberal, lavish, bountiful, plentiful, copious.

What a magnificent bunch of words! They even feel and sound opulent and voluptuous!

Being generous is simply being a giver. To give means to confer ownership of something in return for nothing. It certainly means being unselfish and often involves sacrifice.

Being generous is about preferring others, thinking of their needs before your own. It's also about sharing freely of yourself and what you have. It's the opposite of egotism, greed and selfishness.

Having a generous spirit is to be giving of all that you have and are. It's a spirit that enriches, enlivens and enlarges at every turn. John Wesley summed up the generous spirit in this statement: *"Do all the good you can, by all the means you can, in all the ways you can, in all the places you can, at all the times you can, to all the people you can, as long as ever you can."*

The generous spirit is comprised of four parts:
> Generous mouth - speaks well of, speaks positively, speaks life
> Generous eye - sees the positive, sees the best, is optimistic
> Generous heart - gives freely of emotional warmth and support
> Generous hand - gives freely of finances, physical effort

When we hear the word generosity, most of us immediately think of money. But a generous spirit is not limited to finance and physical goods. Anything God has given us, we can be generous with. We have time, talent and treasure. We have intelligence and emotion, strength and vision. We have life itself.

When you stop giving and offering to the rest of the world, it's time to turn out the lights.

GEORGE BURNS

No person was ever honoured for what he received. Honour has been the reward for what he gave.

CALVIN COOLIDGE, AMERICAN PRESIDENT

WHAT CAN I GIVE?

We all have the potential to be incredibly generous! We just need to be aware of what we can give. Here is a partial list of the gifts that flow from a generous spirit:

> *encouragement and praise, smiles*
> *recognition - credit where it's due*
> *mercy, grace, the benefit of the doubt*
> *respect*
> *trust*
> *commitment, loyalty*
> *friendship*
> *space*
> *verbalised support and confidence in people*
> *significance*
> *success*
> *love*
> *acceptance*
> *security*
> *hope*
> *constructive ideas*
> *forgiveness (Lk 6:38)*
> *sympathy, empathy*
> *finance and material things*
> *time*

How could I unleash generosity in my life? How can I be more of a blessing to those around me?

_____

_____

_____

_____

_____

Blessed are those who can give without remembering and take without forgetting.

ELIZABETH BIBESCO

Love each other with genuine affection, and take delight in honouring each other.

ROMANS 12:10

GOD'S GENEROSITY

The Bible reveals to us who God is, and what He is like. One of the most significant things we discover is that He is GENEROUS. Consider God's generosity in giving Jesus to die for the world's sins.[9] In Pastor Allan Meyer's words, *"God bankrupted Heaven for us"*. Paul wrote, *"Thank God for his Son - a gift too wonderful for words!"*[10]

Paul's second letter to the Corinthians contains a lengthy passage focussing on this theme.[11] It tells us that God loves cheerful givers. We discover that God is our provider and He will supply our needs and enrich us as we give. We learn that our generosity meets the needs of others, brings glory to God, proves obedience and builds heart connections with others.

In the book of Romans we find that our abilities are intended to be coupled with a generous spirit. *"God has given each of us the ability to do certain things well. So if God has given you the ability to prophesy, speak out when you have faith that God is speaking through you. If your gift is serving others, serve them well. If you are a teacher, do a good job teaching. If your gift is to encourage others, do it! If you have money, share it generously. If God has given you leadership ability, take the responsibility seriously. And if you have a gift for showing kindness to others, do it gladly.*[12]

Jesus said, *"It is more blessed to give than to receive."*[13] And, *"The measure you use for others is the measure that God will use for you".*[14] It is clear then, that generosity is a key theme in God's thoughts.

A GENEROUS NATURE

Here are some observations about the nature of generosity:

1. Generosity is unselfish

Obvious, I know. Generosity requires an outward view, not a self-centred one. Nelson Henderson sums it up in this statement: "*The true meaning of life is to plant trees, under whose shade you do not expect to sit.*" The generous spirit, rather than saying, "What can I get out of this?" says, "What can I offer in this situation?"

Generous people are willing to pay a personal price for team success, and to make sacrifices to see others succeed. They are not egotistical - they are able to share the stage, the glory and the credit. As Philippians 2:3 says, *"Don't be selfish; don't live to make a good impression on others. Be humble, thinking of others as better than yourself."*

2. Generosity is win/win

The Bible tells us to *"Give generously, for your gifts will return to you later."*[15] Leadership expert, John Maxwell echoes, *"Your candle loses nothing when it lights another."*[16] Generosity enriches both the giver and the recipient.

Charlie "Tremendous" Jones, in his book, Life Is Tremendous, says, *"If a person is learning to give whether he gets anything or not, he is really giving. And if you'll give - whether you get anything or not - you always get a greater capacity to give."*[17]

God rewards the generous spirit. Abraham and Lot's wealth and possessions had accumulated to the point that they had to go their separate ways. They needed to choose which part of the land each of them would live in. Abraham was the senior but being a generous man he allowed his nephew Lot to choose and take up residence in the very best part of the land. Interestingly, immediately after this incident, God told Abraham that He would give him all the land he could see.[18] God will see to it that the generous are blessed.

3. Generosity has the power to change people

Victor Borge, the famous musical humourist, said, *"Laughter is the shortest distance between two people."* I believe, however, that the shortest distance between two people is generosity.

Generosity imparts worth, and the confidence to believe in one's worth. Generosity connects people. It builds bridges of trust; makes people feel special, loved, worth something.

Generosity engages, encourages, endears, enhances, enriches, enlivens and enlarges.

4. Generosity is intentional

It's a quality that must be purposely built into our character since human nature is inherently selfish. The Bible says, *"A generous man devises generous plans and by generosity he shall stand."*[19]

5. Generosity is not based on deservedness

The very meaning of generosity is to give lavishly, extravagantly, beyond what is deserved or expected. A generous person is not looking for someone worthy of reward - just someone to bless. Proverbs says, *"Blessed are those who are generous, because they feed the poor."*[20] The generous man, because he has, gives to one who has not.

Generosity flows out of the heart, having its motivation within. It does not need to rely on circumstance or outward motivation to set it in motion.

6. Generosity can not be imposed

I once heard Pastor Brian Houston say, *"Generosity is something you are, more than something you do."* It comes out of your very character. God IS GENEROUS - that's why He acts generously. If you have to be forced to give, you're not giving - that's not generosity!

7. Generosity expands you and your world

When we give we grow. We're stretched, but this stretching makes more room in our life for opportunity, strengthening and blessing. Generous people have an abundance mentality. They know there's more where that came from!

GOLDEN RULE OF GENEROSITY: LIVE TO LOVE! ALWAYS LOOK FOR WAYS TO BLESS OTHERS.

DEVELOPING A GENEROUS SPIRIT

Becoming more generous will be the result of right thinking in relation to what we have, where it comes from and what we should do with it. Here are some thinking approaches that will help develop a generous spirit:

> *Think more about others. Put yourself in their shoes. See through their eyes. When we understand what other people need, want or like, we can begin to give.*
> *Understand that what we have, we have been given by God.*
> *Understand that God is not short of cash (or any other good thing!!)*
> *Be content. Think less about what you want and be grateful for what you have.*
> *Be more concerned about showing favour than receiving it.*
> *Be intentional about sharing your time, talents and treasure.*
> *Understand that God blesses those who are generous.*
> *Understand that God blesses through those who are generous.*

POSITIVITY

One of the core characteristics of a shining nature is to have a positive spin on life. Positive people are energising to be around. Their disposition is enthusiastic, optimistic and bright. Their very presence inspires and motivates others. Perhaps it is because they are looking for *"what is true and honourable and right. Think[ing] about things that are pure and lovely and admirable. Think[ing] about things that are excellent and worthy of praise."* [21]

Positive people are outward focussed. They are not consumed by their own issues, constantly being the bearers of their own bad news. Rather, they always have something good to say. They always bring light to a situation. I read a line in a book by Kevin Gerald that puts it beautifully: *"Don't curse the darkness, light a candle."*

A positive spirit is what powers both enthusiasm and encouragement. Let's look at these two traits separately.

POSITIVITY

Do I practise being optimistic?

Do I ask myself what's the best that can happen?

What actions could I take to become a more positive person?

ENTHUSIASM
The Power Of Enthusiasm

Enthusiasm is a powerful force. It creates energy within a person, and it creates energy in the people around that person. Enthusiasm is contagious. It inspires confidence. It motivates an individual and those around him. Enthusiasm and passion are great persuaders.

This is what my pastor, Philip Baker, has to say about it. *"Enthusiasm ... sees things from a different perspective. It takes the hum-drum of every day existence and injects it with vitality and vibe. ... Enthusiasm has this ability to make the ordinary wonderful."*[22] Enthusiasm can really put a shine on life.

Passion is fuel that propels us and gives us the energy to reach our destination. Enthusiasm fires the soul! It gets things done! As Pastor Jack Haynes says, *"The fire of God in your heart will melt the lead in your butt!"* Enthusiasm is visible to those around us. *"If people around you don't see your passion, you probably don't have any!"*[23] If you have it, it will show.

Enthusiasm will fire your desire to learn and grow. It releases a positive attitude. It speaks positively - "words of life". It sees good. It sees potential. It sees possibility.

Enthusiasm brings life to any situation. Think about someone who is "the life of the party" - they are the personification of enthusiasm! What good are we when our presence doesn't bring colour and light? As Malcolm Forbes put it, *"People who never get carried away, should be!"*

Igniting Enthusiasm

Enthusiasm does not just fall on you! It's not a feeling that suddenly comes over you. It's not the same as excitement. It's not the same as happiness. It doesn't come from what happens to you or the circumstances you find yourself in.

The word enthusiasm comes from the Greek, *en theos*, literally meaning, God within. Enthusiasm is an attitude - it comes from within. It comes from understanding and believing in your purpose. It springs from faith and from believing that life, your life, is worthwhile.

Being an attitude, enthusiasm is chosen. We must choose to approach life with enthusiasm. Your character will really begin to shine when you can be enthusiastic even though circumstances are against you.

ENCOURAGEMENT

If light radiates from our life it is going to affect others. If we shine, then what we do and who we are should light up the lives of those around us. Encouragement is a character trait that will do just that.

To encourage means to give hope or confidence to. It literally means, "to put courage into". Webster's Dictionary defines courage as, *"Quality of mind or spirit that enables one to face difficulty, danger and pain with firmness and resolve."* To inspire is similar, meaning to infuse with confidence or resolution.

Encouragement is given; it's a gift. You don't lose anything by giving it, in fact, both parties win. The giver and the receiver will both be enriched.

Don't ever underestimate the awesome power of encouragement. It changes lives! George M. Adams called encouragement *"oxygen to the soul".*

ENCOURAGEMENT

List as many people as you can think of who have believed in you and encouraged you in some way on your journey (even if it was only once, or it was only small!)

1. _____
2. _____
3. _____
4. _____
5. _____
6. _____
7. _____
8. _____
9. _____
10. _____

Write a Thank You card to at least one of these people.
Write an encouraging card to someone you believe in.

The Encouragement Effect

Encouragement enlarges people and builds them up, helping them feel good about themselves. It brings out the best in people and causes them to respond favourably. Henry Ford believed, *"My best friend is the one who brings out the best in me."*

Encouragement draws people together and builds a connection between them. William A. Ward mused, *"Flatter me, and I may not believe you. Criticize me, and I may not like you. Ignore me, and I may not forgive you. Encourage me, and I will not forget you"*. Encouragement helps people feel significant and valued.

Positive support gives confidence and helps people believe in themselves. Encouragement gives hope and brings a positive outlook, helping people persevere through hard times. It builds faith and helps them believe in what they do, giving them the strength to complete difficult tasks.

Affirming words or actions help catapult people toward their potential. Donald O. Clifton & Paula Nelson noted in their book, Soar With Your Strengths: *"In our experience, we have never seen a person who has suffered from over-recognition. People may be damaged by being manipulated with flattery, but it may be impossible to give too much praise for achievement. If it was possible, the likes of Bob Hope should have been destroyed long ago. Instead, they seem to get better and better."*[24]

Knowing that others believe in us and support us motivates us and spurs us on to action. It also helps us to believe in others, opening our eyes to the good in them. It builds trust and belief in each other, and in doing so builds team spirit.

When a people feel encouraged they can be bold and do what they otherwise could not or would not do. They can face the impossible and overcome incredible adversity. They feel as if their spirit is renewed and they've been given fresh courage.

Developing an Encouraging Nature

Some people have a special gift of encouragement. They build people up and give them courage every time they open their mouth - without even thinking about it. They are amazing people to be around.

The rest of us have to cultivate this skill and it's important that we do. Encouragement is a major player in leadership and teamwork. It's like fuel in that it gives energy, and it's like oil in that it keeps things smooth.

Let's be encouragers! Those who encourage are the ones who are given permission to influence and lead people. That's what shining is all about!

GOLDEN RULE OF POSITIVITY: APPROACH LIFE WITH THE INTENTION OF INSPIRING EVERYONE.

Kind words can be short and easy to speak, but their echoes are truly endless.

Mother Teresa

People will forget what you said, people will forget what you did, but people will never forget how you made them feel.

Maya Angelou

169

DEVELOPING AN ENCOURAGING NATURE

How do you encourage others? Here are some great starting points:
> *Speak well of them in the presence of others.*
> *Tell them when they do well.*
> *Send notes and cards with messages that build them up.*
> *Call them for no other reason than to tell them that you're thinking of them, that they're great, that you appreciate them!*
> *Pray with them.*
> *Pray for them and let them know.*
> *Let them know you support them - verbally or by helping them in some practical way.*
> *Thank people when they help or bless you.*
> *Praise the positive at every opportunity.*
> *Believe in them and make sure they know it.*
> *Be a person with a positive disposition.*
> *Be an outstanding example!*

RESPECT

A person of great character will be someone who respects others. To respect means to consider worthy of high regard; to treat with esteem; or to defer to.

Generally respect is earned. As people prove themselves to be worthy or deserving, we begin to respect them. More importantly though, respect is given. You can give it or not give it, it's your choice. A person of character chooses to give respect to any person regardless of their ability to prove worth or significance.

Respect is based on what we believe about people, so it is important that we base our beliefs on the truth. First, people are created by God. That alone makes them significant and worthwhile. They are created in the image of God. That means they have awesome potential, potential we can't even begin to imagine. We know that He loves each one just as much as the other, and that each has a purpose, a future and a hope. If we can keep these truths in mind, that's a pretty good start! We respect people when we value them.

Your respect for people will be made visible in the way you talk to them and treat them. Your tone of voice, body language and choice of words will tell others whether you value them or not.

Respect for others can also be enhanced by learning to "put yourself in their shoes." When we can change our perspective and see a situation through the eyes of another, we will often have a much greater understanding of who they are and why they do what they do. We then respond to them more thoughtfully and with more empathy. We can show them that we believe their feelings, fears and ideas - even though they may be different to ours - are valid and significant.

When we show respect for others we will find that they develop respect for us too.

THE GOLDEN RULE OF RESPECT: SHOW RESPECT TO EVERYONE, ALWAYS.

A RESPECTER OF PERSONS

Ask yourself these questions and then discuss them honestly with a friend to get an objective view.
1. *Do I treat all people with the same level of respect?*
2. *Do some people deserve more respect than others? Why?*
3. *What determines the level of respect I offer people?*
4. *Do I judge people by their appearance?*
5. *Is my respect based on who they seem to be or who made them?*
6. *What makes me feel respected?*
7. *Who do I know that respects me? Why do they respect me?*

COURAGE

There are many images that come to mind when one thinks of the concept of courage. There's the six-year-old brushing himself off, blood trickling from his knee as he picks himself up off the asphalt, biting hard on his lip and blinking his eyes. There's the fresh-faced private charging into battle as the bullets spray around him. There's a teenage girl with newly fitted braces making her way through the stares and the whispers to her locker, determined that this is not going to ruin her life. There's a boy saying "no" at an end of year party with all his mates. You may think of Christopher Reeves who, as a quadriplegic, was determined to make a difference in

Be kind, for everyone you meet is fighting a great battle.

PHILO OF ALEXANDRIA

Courage is resistance to fear, mastery of fear-not absence of fear. Except a creature be part coward it is not a compliment to say it is brave.

MARK TWAIN

the world in his lifetime. Or, maybe the artist or musician who stares the fear of failure in the face and tries anyway.

We need courage to face all the world throws at us. Adversity and challenge are unavoidable facts of life. They come whether we're prepared or not and we don't know how or when they'll force themselves upon us. Courage helps us to stand firm through them, and also helps us to prepare for them.

Courage is needed to face testing circumstances or difficult people. It is also needed to confront our own inadequacies and make positive changes in our lives. We need courage to deal with major personal issues. It takes courage to follow hard after our calling and to pursue our full potential. Why? Because the path of destiny is an exciting one but not an easy one. As the great dreamer, Walt Disney said, *"All our dreams can come true - if we have the courage to pursue them."*

Courage reveals itself when we choose to do what needs to be done or what is right, knowing full well there will be a cost to us. It makes itself evident when, in the face of pain or difficulty, we choose to do the right thing anyway. Courage grits its teeth and does it regardless.

Courage does not exist without adversity, opposition, difficulty or danger. Courage is not found in the absence of fear or obstacles, for there it is unnecessary. Rather, it is found standing firm or pressing forward in spite of them. As it has been said, *"Feel the fear and do it anyway!"*

Courage is a quality that enables us to proceed with certainty in the face of possible danger and potential pain. It will help us get back up when we've been knocked down. It will help us deal with whatever may come our way, knowing that we have a life worth living, a future worth fighting for, and a light that was created to shine!

THE GOLDEN RULE OF COURAGE: DO WHAT'S RIGHT, IN SPITE OF EVERYTHING.

Our character is the representation of our heart. Let's be committed to building it strong and pure and to guard it with our life. Great character will allow us to shine brilliantly from the inside out.

Character cannot be developed in ease and quiet. Only through experience of trial and suffering can the soul be strengthened, ambition inspired, and success achieved.

HELEN KELLER

The ultimate measure of a man is not where he stands in moments of comfort, but where he stands at times of challenge and controversy.

MARTIN LUTHER KING, JR.

prayer

Magnificent God, You are awesome and Your character is perfect. Please show me more of Your amazing heart and help me to become more like You. Show me what needs to change in me. I truly want to be someone whose inner life shines. Amen.

contract
Commitment To Character

I, _____, am committed to being a person whose core is strong and able to support an expansive and effective outer life. I will continually and diligently work on my character, relentlessly pursuing a pure heart. I will put myself in positions of accountability to ensure I don't lose sight of this goal.

Signature _____   Date _____

ENDNOTES

1. Noland, Rory: *The Heart Of The Artist*; Zondervan Publishing House, Grand Rapids, MI; 1999, p14.
2. Strand, Robert: *Success without Guilt*; New Leaf Press, Green Forest, AR; 1997: p87.
3. John Maxwell & Jim Dornan: *Becoming a Person of Influence*; Thomas Nelson Publishers, Nashville; 1997, p24.
4. Maxwell, John: *Be A People Person*, Victor Books, Wheaton IL; 1994, p121.
5. Psalm 50:10-12
    For all the animals of the forest are mine,
     and I own the cattle on a thousand hills.
    Every bird of the mountains
    and all the animals of the field belong to me.
    If I were hungry, I would not mention it to you,
    for all the world is mine and everything in it.

    Psalm 24:1
    The earth is the Lord's, and everything in it.
    The world and all its people belong to Him.

    1 Corinthians 8:6 (NLT)
    But we know there is only one God, the Father, who created everything, and we exist for Him.
6. Luke 11:10
7. Galatians 6:4
8. See Parable of the Talents, Matthew 25:14-30; Romans 12:6-11; Galatians 6:4-5; 1 Timothy 4:12,14-15 be an example, and, stir up the gift.
9. John 3:16
10. 2 Corinthians 9:15
11. 2 Corinthians 9:7-15. (The generosity theme actually begins at the beginning of Chapter 8.)
    "… God loves the person who gives cheerfully. And God will generously provide all you need. Then you will always have everything you need and plenty left over to share with others. As the Scriptures say,
    "Godly people give generously to the poor.
    Their good deeds will never be forgotten."
    For God is the one who gives the seed to the farmer and then bread to eat. In the same way, he will give you many opportunities to do good, and he will produce a great harvest of generosity in you.
    Yes, you will be enriched so that you can give even more generously. And when we take your gifts to those who need them, they will break out in thanksgiving to God. So two good things happen - the needs of the Christians in Jerusalem will be met, and they will joyfully express their thanksgiving to God. You will be glorifying God through your generous gifts. For your generosity to them will prove that you are obedient to the

Good News of Christ. And they will pray for you with deep affection because of the wonderful grace of God shown through you.

12. Romans 12:6-8
13. Acts 20:35
14. Luke 6:38
15. Ecclesiastes 11:1
16. Maxwell, John C.: *The 21 Indispensible Qualities Of A Leader*; Thomas Nelson Publishers, Nashville; 1999, p58.
17. Jones, Charlie "Tremendous": *Life Is Tremendous*; Living Books, Tyndale House Publishers, Inc., Wheaton, IL; 1968, p38.
18. Genesis 13:5-11
19. Isaiah 32:8 NKJV
20. Proverbs 22:9
21. Philippians 4:8
22. Baker, Philip: *Attitudes of Amazing Achievers*; Webb & Partners, Perth, Australia; 2000, p94.
23. Pastor Wayne Alcorn, Brisbane City Church. Queensland, Australia.
24. Clifton, Donald O. & Nelson, Paula: *Soar With Your Strengths*; Dell Publishing, New York, NY; 1992, p178.

community

a place to shine

RELATIONSHIP

We all live in community. No one can survive in life without interaction with other human beings. We were never meant to be isolated. Thinker and philosopher Ralph Waldo Emerson said, *"All are needed by each one: Nothing is fair or good alone."* God Himself said, *"It is not good for … man to be alone."*[1] We were designed for relationship - both with God and with people.

God initiated a relationship with humans by creating us, and the Bible tells us that He is passionate about His relationship with us.[2] This is clearly demonstrated by the lengths He took to make it possible for us to have a relationship with Him. He gave His only Son to die, to pay the price for our sins - the sins that kept us separated from Him. This is how eager God is for us to know Him.

People are also designed for interaction with each other. Although technology is making it easier to do things without actual human contact, it is still people who make these technological systems work. And these systems are put to work for the benefit of people. Our lives are inextricably intertwined.

Jesus said the greatest commandment is to love God; the second greatest, to love people. He meant for us to live not only for ourselves, but also for others.

Our work and our art should not be produced purely for the profit it will bring to our own world. It should also be motivated out of the potential for increase to others; the possibility of encouragement, enrichment, support and inspiration; the opportunity to amuse, entertain or inspire delight; the chance to teach, motivate or provoke enlightened thought.

Relationship brings richness and variety, sometimes pain and frustration, but - most of all - meaning to life. What is recognition without relationship? What is celebration without someone to celebrate with? How do we encourage, share, or show respect without another being the focus of our attention? How can we demonstrate integrity, humility, or generosity if there is no relationship to draw it out of us? Interaction with people provides the conditions required for building character.

Relationships and life's experiences are also fuel for our art. They are the most fertile source of material for our work. Relationship brings meaning to our work. It gives us something to write, paint, play, sing and dance about. It gives us something to comment on. It gives us ideas to make relatable to an audience. When we understand this, our work has the incredible potential to bring meaning to our relationships.

Our community, then, gives us a context for our creativity, an environment in which to both cultivate and express our gifts. Our community is made up of all those we have relationship with as well as those with whom we have the potential for relationship. As Pastor of one of North America's largest churches, Rick Warren says, *"We are created for community, fashioned for fellowship, and formed for a family, and none of us can fulfil God's purposes by ourselves."*[3]

CHURCH

The simplest definition of the Church is; *the community of believers.* The New Testament alludes to this community in two ways. One is the universal communion of believers across all the earth and through all of history. The other is the more specific gathering of a local group of believers.

Although salvation is for us individually, the Christian life is not meant to be a solitary affair. As Pastor Rick Warren says, *"While your relationship to Christ is personal, God never intends it to be private."* The Bible tells us, *"Let us not give up the habit of meeting together."*[4] When we are "born again", it is into God's family. Every Christian needs to belong to a local church.

We are meant to be committed to this group and actively involved in it. When we do so we begin to shine bright as our own lives are enriched and in turn we enrich those around us. Being an active church member grows us in so many ways. Here are just a few:

We are in a position to receive great teaching and to strengthen our knowledge and faith. We grow in character as we learn to serve, accept, forgive and be devoted to each other. Our character is further formed as we make ourselves accountable and submit to those in authority over us. We find friendship and we encourage and build each other up in faith. We have a safe place to discover our gifts, and grow in the expression of them. We sharpen our skills in a positive, nurturing environment. It is the best place on the planet for developing both our gifts and our character. We learn to give. We learn to love. We learn to truly live!

The church is God's idea. *"He created the church to meet your five deepest needs: a purpose to live for, people to live with, principles to live by, a profession to live out, and power to live on. There is no other place on earth where you can find all five of these benefits in one place."*[5]

Involvement in your local Rotary Club or Sports Club will provide some of these benefits to a degree, but it will never be able to develop and grow you holistically the way a healthy church can.

CHURCH AND CREATIVE PEOPLE

Unfortunately, many creative and artistic people have given up on the Church in the last Century. They've felt misunderstood and unable to fit in, sometimes even being clearly ostracised. However, this is not the way it's supposed to be: The Church needs creative people and creative people need the Church.

It has been exciting to see many relevant and accepting churches spring up over the earth in the last few decades. Please don't give up on the Church! While there are some legalistic, irrelevant and weird examples out there, the majority are full of normal and good-hearted people. *You belong in God's household with every other Christian.*[6] You need the church and the church needs you.

As we commit to our local church we are given an environment in which to flourish. I believe Psalm 1:3 applies to those who truly make this commitment;

> *They are like trees planted along the riverbank,*
> *bearing fruit each season without fail.*
> *Their leaves never wither,*
> *and in all they do, they prosper.*

You are called to belong, not just believe.

Rick Warren

Talents were given primarily so that we might have a glorious means of praising Him, as we offer our gifts back to their source.

Patrick Kavanaugh

BEING A LIGHTHOUSE

Our relationship with the church community should be fueling us, refining us, stoking up the fire so that when we are out in the larger community we are equipped to shine and make a difference. We were never meant to live out our lives exclusively within the walls of our church community. We live in a large and often dark world. Our light is meant to bring some illumination to that world.

SECULAR AND SACRED

Sometime in the early Middle Ages a view of life and spirituality formed that was not based on Biblical truth. The clergy were seen as spiritual and "higher" than everyone else. There began to be an increasing distinction between the secular and sacred. Spirituality became something that was separate to the rest of life - somehow above the ordinary living of life. It was something mystical and unattached to the practical living out of Christian principles. It became purely religious.

We are created as spiritual beings - there's no getting away from that. Because of our need as humans to define and name things we have come up with different ways to label our experience of life. The ancient Greeks came up with the three basic divisions of Body, Soul and Spirit. While this is helpful sometimes, our tendency to compartmentalise has seen us all too often treat these as totally discrete aspects. It then becomes easy to believe one part is more significant than another. The truth is, no part of life is more spiritual than another.

Let's look at an example. When we are physically very tired, our emotions are affected. We probably won't be able to think well, and we lose the ability to focus. This could affect our ability to connect with God (although not His ability to connect with us!). So we see that in a person the physical, emotional, mental and spiritual are inextricably intertwined. God has created us as whole beings and deals with us as such.

The Apostle Paul wrote, *"Take your everyday, ordinary life - your sleeping, eating, going-to-work, and walking-around life - and place it before God as an offering.*[7] *This is your spiritual act of worship.*"[8] It is clear that as a Christian, whatever we do in life, wherever we go, whomever we do it with - it's all part of living for God.

Once we see this on a personal level it is also important to see it at the level of community. The objects of God's affection are people - all people. God sent Jesus to die because He loved the world.[9] It's not only Christians

Be the change you wish to see in the world.

Gandhi

When we hurt ourselves, others are always affected. The converse is also true. When we choose to do what is right, what is true, what is good, it always bleeds over into the lives of others.

Erwin Raphael McManus

God is interested in, it's everyone. He is passionate about pursuing those far from Him and one of the main ways He does that is through Christians who take their light and shine it directly into lost lives.

If we view any place outside the church as secular we risk "hiding our lamp under a bushel"[10]. If work is not sacred we may leave our light at home. If the pub is secular we may never go there. If the local football club is not sacred we may not join. If the university is unholy we may choose not to go. But where are the people our light is meant to shine on?

The whole Universe was made by God. The Bible says, *"everything comes from Him; everything exists by his power and is intended for his glory."*[11] As writer, film-maker and artist, Franky Schaeffer, wrote, *"There is no Christian world, no secular world; these are just words. There is only one world - the world God made."*

ILLUMINATE

Write down the two places (communities) where your light is most effective.

_____

_____

Are there other places where it could be more effective? Are there any circumstances or environments in which you may be hiding your light under a bushel?

_____

_____

_____

_____

SERVICE

We are meant to make a contribution to our community, not just consume from it. Where and how we can make the best and most meaningful contribution is only discovered over time as we serve in different areas and develop maturity and perspective.

"You discover your role in life through relationships with others."[13] Every encounter teaches us something and all our experiences shape us. We

find out what we're good at by getting involved and serving. Pretty soon our areas of giftedness will begin to show.

Through service, our abilities develop and gain meaning and we discover a sense of significance as our efforts make a difference for others. Also, interaction with others gives us opportunity to grow in character, further increasing our potential to be a blessing.

Creativity coach, Julia Cameron, writes;

> Chekhov advised actors, "If you want to work on your career, work on yourself." It might equally be advised, if you want to work on yourself, work to make your career of service to something larger than yourself. Dedicate yourself to something or someone other than yourself. This expansion will make you larger as a person and as an artist."[14]

Some of the greatest and most respected people ever to have lived knew this principle. The first to spring to mind is Mother Theresa of Calcutta. Of course, there are many others... Ghandi, Martin Luther King Jr., Albert Einstein...

As Ghandi said, *"The best way to find yourself is to lose yourself in service to others."* If you have not yet found exactly what you were made for, begin by looking for opportunities to serve. Ask yourself, "What can I get involved in that will be a blessing to others?" You may not find your perfect role first time out, but you will definitely come across some sign-posts to head you in the right direction and you will have begun down the path of discovery and fulfilment.

TEAM

One great expression of community and a model of the larger community, is a team. Teamwork is simply organised cooperation. A team is a collection of people working together. They have a common goal, they cooperate with each other, they communicate with each other and they commit to each other and the common goal.

One of the qualities of people who shine in their community is eagerness to be a valuable team member. It is the ability to be unselfish and altruistic, putting ego aside and bringing whatever contribution one is able to bring to the team. It is being willing to do whatever is required and playing to make the team great.

Once when I was thinking about the kind of people that would make up my dream team, I made the following notes:

A dream team member is one who;
> cares about the others, respecting them and encouraging them, spurring them on to greater heights;
> understands the team's purpose and the importance of its role and accepts responsibility for it, putting it above his or her own agenda;
> values excellence and is eager to develop his or her gift, becoming more competent and confident every week;
> is enthusiastic and generous, always prepared to go the extra mile;
> is fully committed to all of the above, and has a heart that is passionate for God.

Great team players are those who understand the value of team and know how it works. They play by the team rules and standards, and fulfil the team expectations knowing that their success will come with the team's success.

The Bible says, *"Don't think only about your own affairs, but be interested in others, too, and what they are doing."*[15] Great team players make everyone around them feel important and make them look, sound and perform better.

Of course, there are no perfect teams. Some people are great to be around and fun to work with but some people just rub us up the wrong way. They don't know how to make the team experience a good one. However, even these people's presence in a team has purpose - to give us the opportunity to grow!

Team

The word TEAM can be thought of as an acronym for, Together Each Achieves More:

TOGETHER

The most important concept relating to team is "togetherness". Many have said it is better to have a champion team than a team full of champions who can't work together. A whole bunch of individuals pulling in different directions will never get anything done. This would be worse than one person trying to do the whole job alone.

In a team we come together, unified by a vision and common purpose. The team is a place of encouragement, safety and support because we are in agreement. We communicate, cooperate and pool our resources. We're in it together. We work together, we succeed together, we win together.

EACH
Though we are part of a team we are all expected to contribute. Although we are accountable to the team, we must accept personal responsibility to bring value. Each individual brings his or her own unique gifts and this gives diversity and strength to the team. We need to see the big picture and know our part in it.

ACHIEVES
The team has a mission. It is expected that we will see results as we act intentionally and pursue growth.

MORE
Two are better than one. A three-stranded cord is not easily broken.[16] When we act together there is a greater capacity for results. The potential increases exponentially as synergy begins to come into play. Compared to the energy of one person alone, the energy of a group of people in agreement can be astounding.

PEOPLE PEOPLE

If life is so dependent on relationships, then success in life will require that I learn to be a "people person".

Questions to ponder:
1. *Are you a pleasure to be around?*
2. *Think about every encounter you've had with people in the last 2 days. Are the lives of others enlarged just because you are in their world?*
3. *Do you inspire the best in people?*
4. *In what ways are people benefited when you use your gifts?*
5. *Are you intentionally being a valuable contributor to your particular community?*

COMMUNICATION

More than just talking and hearing, communication is about expressing, listening, perceiving, understanding. It's about the sharing of thoughts and feelings. It's about togetherness.

Communication is always two-way; there's transmission and reception. However, one who is skilled at it can stimulate the process and bring "communion" more readily.

We all love skilful communicators. Somehow they make us understand - and at the same time feel understood. They make us feel comfortable - with them and with ourselves. They make us feel significant - worth the effort of sharing time with.

It is certainly well worth the effort to develop some skill in the area of communication. Learning to express clearly is key. Our expression is the lens through which our light reaches the world, so the better our communication, the clearer and brighter we shine.

Good "transmitters" are candid about their ideas and open about their feelings. They are honest about who they are, and confident enough to accept who they are. Good transmitters are direct. They don't beat around the bush but communicate honestly and clearly. They are also thoughtful, not quick to speak, always keeping in mind the other persons and their positions.

Learning to be a good receiver will also expand the scope and effectiveness of all our relationships.

Our lives are shaped by a multitude of factors. Are we male or female? Where did we grow up? What country, what city, town, neighbourhood? What kind of education? What was the relationship with our parents like? Did we have any traumas or stressful life experiences? And on and on it goes. All these experiences and factors colour the way we see life, and therefore the way we listen and express.

Naturally, we perceive life through the filter of what we already know. Everyone does, and everyone has a different filter. An incredibly helpful means of improving communication is simply to put ourselves in other people's shoes. Try to look from behind their eyes. What is their background? What causes them to act or think the way they do? Could they misinterpret what I'm saying here? How do I need to communicate to them?

It's also important to remember that music is a very gregarious thing. It's all about relationships. You can be the greatest artist that has ever lived. But if you don't know how to relate to people and how to communicate, then there you are: the greatest artist that ever lived, playing in your apartment.

SAXOPHONIST, ERNIE WATTS

Interest is the sincerest form of respect.

BARBARA SHER

When we take this approach it brings us insight and empathy. We begin to understand them.

It shows people that we respect them, and that we have cared enough to consider their position and how they arrived at it. The results are that we build trust and foster openness. This brings an ease to the relationship and promotes self-esteem in those with whom we are communicating.

It is good to remember that perhaps the greatest gift we can give another is the gift of attention. When we show our interest, listen well, ask good questions to clarify, and give thoughtful responses, people feel valued. That's the foundation for rich and rewarding relationships.

CLEAR TRANSMISSION AND RECEPTION

Are you learning to communicate skilfully?
Take the following thoughts and discuss them with a friend.

A good transmitter
> *Sends clear messages (speaks openly, honestly and directly)*
> *Optimises the transmission for the receiver*

A good receiver
> *Asks good questions*
> *Responds thoughtfully*
> *Listens actively*

Which areas of communication are your strongest?

_____

_____

_____

_____

Which are your weakest?

_____

_____

_____

Our community will provide us with every opportunity to shine. We must be good stewards not only of our talents, but also of the environments and relationships we have been given. Our gifts should enhance the lives of our neighbours and workmates. Our presence should enrich the experience for everyone. In God's economy we are blessed to be a blessing.

The point of life is learning to love - God and people. Life minus love equals zero.

RICK WARREN

I sincerely believe that the word relationships is the key to the prospect of a decent world. It seems abundantly clear that every problem you will have - in your family, in your work, in our nation, or in this world - is essentially a matter of relationships, of interdependence.

CLARENCE FRANCIS

prayer

Dear God, thank you for initiating a relationship with me. Please help me to be a lover of God and a lover of people. Teach me how to give of myself and touch others, enriching my community through Your love and grace. Amen.

contract
Commitment To Community

I, _____, understand the vital importance of relationships and strong community. I commit to being an active and valuable member of every community I am a part of. I will be an intentional and enthusiastic contributor and a grateful beneficiary.

Signature _____ Date _____

ENDNOTES

1. Genesis 2:18
2. Exodus 34:14
3. Rick Warren, *The Purpose Driven Life*, Zondervan, Grand Rapids, MI, 2002, p130.
4. Hebrews 10:25, *TEV*
5. Rick Warren, *The Purpose Driven Life*, Zondervan, Grand Rapids, Michigan; 2002, p132.
6. Ephesians 2:19b *Living Bible*
7. Romans 12:1 *The Message*
8. Romans 12:1 *NIV*
9. John 3:16
10. Luke 8:16
11. Romans 11:36
12. Schaeffer, Franky; *Addicted To Mediocrity; 20th Century Christians And The Arts*: Crossway Books, Wheaton, IL; 1981, p47.
13. Warren, Rick: *The Purpose Driven Life*, Zondervan, Grand Rapids, MI, 2002, p131.
14. Cameron, Julia: *Walking In This World*; Rider, London, www.randomhouse.co.uk; 2002, p268.
15. Phillippians 2:4
16. Ecclesiastes 4:12

permission to shine

PERMISSION TO SHINE

Congratulations on reading this far! By now you should be thoroughly convinced that your life should have its own unique glow and that the light and colour you radiate should inspire and touch those around you. Your life can, and should, make a difference.

God's plans for us are exceedingly good, but they don't come to pass unless we take up the responsibility of living out our calling. We need to discover our gifts and develop them, cultivating competence and confidence. We need to continually grow, not just in what we do, but also in who we are, developing character in our lives. All this takes place in the context of our community, in the day to day hustle of life, amidst the interactions we have with the people we do life with.

Of course, none of this is instant. It's a journey - sometimes scenic and stimulating, other times dry, gruelling, challenging or just plain boring. Every step of the path has its purpose and prepares us for what is to come. We grow in patience and perseverance, and develop useful habits, attitudes and effective approaches to life.

Take Your Dream And Live It!

The dreams God placed in your heart are not to be ignored, but fleshed out and fulfilled. Don't be afraid to follow them - they will both fuel and satisfy you. They are meant to draw you into a pursuit that will grow and develop you.

Many of us are frustrated by, or fearful of, the dream in our heart. This is because these God-planted dreams are too big for us. We cannot fulfil them as we are - we need to grow into them and this takes courage. We must become the person who can live out those dreams. It is possible, and we must do it. I hope this book has helped you discover how to become the person who can live out your dreams.

My parting advice to you is - Be faithful to God and His ways and be diligent about becoming the person you were made to be.

Our lives are for the glory of God. They are meant to be glorious! Live to Shine! Don't hide the lamp! Shine in every community you are part of and openly give God the glory! Light up your corner of the world! You have permission!

Shine On!
Mark

"Trust in the Lord and do good. Then you will live safely in the land and prosper. Take delight in the Lord, and He will give you your heart's desires. Commit everything you do to the Lord. Trust Him, and He will help you."

PSALM 37:3-5